£4.50

F2

Collector's guide to Militaria

Collector's guide to Militaria

Derek E. Johnson

WILLIAM LUSCOMBE

First published in Great Britain by
William Luscombe Publisher Ltd
The Mitchell Beazley Group
Artists House
14–15 Manette Street
London, W1V 5LB
1976

ISBN 0 86002 096 7

Printed in Great Britain by Pitman Press Ltd, Bath
Phototypeset by Tradespools Ltd, Frome, Somerset

To Chick
My inspiration and mainstay

Acknowledgements

My thanks to fellow-collectors, dealers and museums who allowed me full run of their treasured pieces, and without whose help this book could have never been finished.

First and foremost, my heartfelt thanks to James W. Schaaf of Concord, USA, who spent many long hours over a great many of the excellent illustrations; to Arnold Chernoff and AA White Engravers Inc., USA, for information and illustration of the Colt bronze; to George B. Harris III for illustrations of US awards; to Mr & Mrs Farnell-Watson for allowing me to photograph a selection of their 500-plus Britain's soldiers; to David Johnson for the loan of the Elcho bayonet; to David Clarke, curator of Colchester Castle Museum; and to Victor S. Wilson S.P.R., A.I.L., for German/English translations.

Contents

Illustrations

Credits for photographs

The author's thanks are due to the following for permission to reproduce the photographs illustrating this book: James W. Schaaf collection: Nos. 1, 4, 5, 55, 56, 57, 58, 59, 62, 63, 64; John M. Graham collection: Nos. 2, 6; George Repaire collection: No. 7; Keeble collection: Nos. 9, 10, 11, 12, 50; Mick Brown collection: No. 15; Roger Perryman collection: No. 18; Farnell-Watson collection: Nos. 24, 25; Arnold Chernoff & A.A. White Engravers Inc.; No. 28; Colchester Castle Museum collection: Nos. 38, 39, 40; David Johnson collection: No. 44; John Krivine: No. 46; David Ashton collection: No. 51; George B. Harris III collection: Nos. 60, 61.

Introduction

War always has been, and always will be, an evil force, but, no matter how Man strives to control his primaeval urges or re-channel his aggressive feeling, that indefinable instinct which burns deep within his soul will, from time to time, explode and overflow. So much akin to a slumbering volcano, Man, for all his twentieth century know-how and thin veneer of civilisation, just has to explode and give vent to his feelings with a blood-letting – be it the back-streets of Chicago or New York or the deserts of the Middle East or the jungles of Vietnam or Korea – murder and warfare in one form or another still rage on. Through the ages there have been many bloody wars and battles, and the weapons and equipment of these conflicts make for an interesting study . . . hence the great upsurge in all matters pertaining to militaria.

In the following chapters, the reader will journey through a strange and wonderful world crowded with items that can be traced far back into the annals of history. With each new piece obtained, whether it is a mere brass button, cap badge or faded photograph, we learn a little more of the complex history of militaria. For example, who would have thought that when that gallant World War 1 flying ace, Ernst Udet, gave some small keepsakes to the Schaaf family way back in 1933, he was also leaving a link with a political regime (the NSDAP) that was to turn the world upside-down!

Some collectors will spend a life-time searching for a particular item, George Repaire's choice selection of Colts and the George B. Harris III medal collection being but a couple of examples. Others will collect almost anything with a military flavour, filling their den or study with all manner of strange and varied items. To be a collector of anything is a visible mark of idiosyncracy, so those about to march into the strange world of militaria should get used to the odd looks and comments of friends and relations!

Before starting on this collecting business, it would be as well to visit your local bookshop or library and peruse the list of reference works. Read, study, and digest all the books that you can find on this particular hobby, for only by learning through other folk's mistakes and experience can you ever hope to build a worthwhile collection. Try to visit some of the museums listed in the Appendix, for actually *looking* at the pieces about which you have read is always a great help.

Good collecting!

Derek E. Johnson
Pennyfarthing Antiques,
Clacton, Essex.

1 Antique Firearms and Powder Flasks

When starting a collection of antique firearms, the most important thing to remember is the emphasis on that word *Antique*. It is all very well reading about the wonderful selection of guns that are available to be collected in such places as America, but here in Great Britain things are somewhat different. Start a collection of modern breech-loaders, semi-automatic pistols or revolvers without the proper certificates or permits and you are likely to find your collecting days rather short and financially painful! To prevent this unhappy ending, a guide to what should and should not be collected can be found later in this chapter.

At some point in his life, every schoolboy (from the age of 7 to 70!), secretly yearns to handle or perhaps even own an old gun, for the shades of Dick Turpin, Jesse James and Long John Silver, complete with brace of smoking pistols, seem to stay with us always. Some of us do more than just read or dream about it, we set out to satisfy that yearning by actually purchasing such a piece.

However, before dashing out and buying any old gun, it is advisable to know what kind of weapon you really want and what kind of price you can expect to pay. If you have set your heart on, say, a silver-mounted, flintlock duelling pistol by one of the better known makers of the 1780s, you can't expect much change from two or three hundred pounds. Then again, if you simply want a flintlock pistol, be it Indian, African or one of the many continental varieties, you should soon be fixed up. A word of warning, however – if you do decide to settle for the latter, make sure

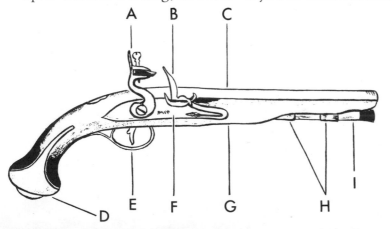

Fig. 1   Flintlock holster pistol *c.* 1790:
A – cock,
B – frizzen,
C – barrel,
D – butt-cap,
E – trigger-guard,
F – lock,
G – stock,
H – ramrod pipes,
I – ramrod

that you are actually buying an antique and not something that has been knocked up in a native bazaar from oddments of old gas barrel and a chair leg! A number of these crude trading pieces are slowly finding their way on to the British market via the increasingly popular package holidays. Bought for about four or five pounds from a stall in Bombay or Fayid, these roughly-built pieces are artificially aged then fobbed off as antique. Those who know their antiques are not taken in, but the greenhorn, who is used to seeing his longed-for piece framed in the display cabinet of a museum or the pages of a glossy magazine, may be caught unawares.

My advice to anyone buying his first few pieces is – take a knowledgeable friend along, go over the offered article with a fine eye-glass, look hard, ask questions, and look again. If the answers are not satisfactory or you're not happy with what you see, then leave well alone. A vendor with nothing to hide will assist in every way he can, even to the point of stripping off the lock-plate; for it is behind here that one can see if the piece has been tampered with. Check for fresh cuts and file marks on the woodwork and around metal. Of course, on many a flintlock or percussion piece,

1. Cased duelling pistols made by Joseph Manton, Berkeley Square, London, 1812–19

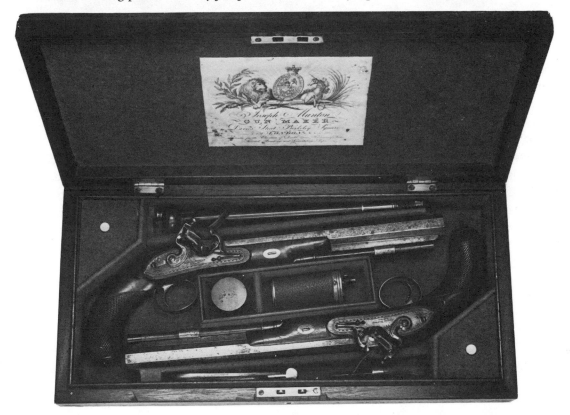

13

2.   LeMat percussion pistol bearing both LeMat and British proof marks! It was brought into Louisiana by a blockade runner during the American Civil War

some repairs may have been carried out on a sear or main spring. These do get broken from time to time, and it is far better to have a working lock with the full-bodied feel of a cock or hammer under tension than one that shakes and clatters like a football rattle. Look instead for freshly drilled holes and cut marks around lock and side-plate. These indicate that a side-nail has been moved or that the lock has been altered or replaced. Look also for alien screws. The screws of a period piece were hand-cut, since all parts of a bespoke piece would be individually tailored.

On most English arms, it was the practice to stamp the barrel with a proof mark. These proof marks which, to the layman, mean little or nothing, convey a great deal to the initiated. Not only do they tell us just where the barrel was proofed, but also, by the size, shape and design of the mark, the date it was stamped. Once again a

Fig. 2   Lock marks: *from left to right* 1810 (George I); 1835 (William IV); 1846 (Victoria); 1793 (East India Company). Stockmark: 1810 (East India Company). Storekeeper's mark: 1837 (Enfield)

3. A member of the Clacton branch of the Muzzle Loaders' Association of Great Britain firing a ·577 two-band Enfield percussion rifle. Note the snap-cap nipple protector hanging beneath the trigger guard

certain amount of care should be exercised when passing a judgement, for it was not uncommon for English barrels – complete with makers' mark and proofs – to find their way over to Europe where they were married-up with Spanish, French or German stocks and furniture.

Just as a collector of fine English silver would expect to find a good set of hall-marks on his choicest piece, then so too would the gun enthusiast expect to find a good set of proofs on his latest find – and with good reason. Way back in the mists of time, when nearly every household sported a firearm of some form or the other, a great number of inferior barrels were shipped into England from foreign parts. Built into cheap and nasty 'off-the-peg' firearms, a great number were prone to bursting once in action. A great clamouring among the leading English gunsmiths brought in an Act which allowed for proofing to show that the barrel in question had passed both a viewing and proofing test at the recognised Proof House. In this way they could prove beyond a shadow of a doubt the identity of an English barrel. The study of proof marks through the ages is most rewarding, and, for further information, one should consult Howard Blackmore's *British Military Firearms, 1650–1850*.

Loading and firing in those times was really something of an art, for gunpowder and ball had to be introduced down the mouth of the barrel – a somewhat hazardous pastime if you were in a rain-storm or in the midst of a raging battle! Although our intrepid muzzle-loader will not have to face hordes of charging fuzzy-wuzzies or ranks of steaming, blood-thirsty cavalrymen today, he still has to contend with

15

the elements and, 'Keep your powder dry!' is still sound advice. Those who wish to pursue the sport of the muzzle-loader can join the Muzzle Loaders Assoc. of Great Britain, for there are active clubs all over Britain where the sound of flint on steel and the smell of burning black powder is all part of a monthly ritual. Full details from the Hon. Secretary (at the time of writing: R. G. Ricketts, 92 Baldwins Lane, Hall Green, Birmingham 28). Enclose a stamped addressed envelope.

For these collectors it is not enough just to find an antique gun, clean it, restore it and then give it pride of place in their den. The joy of actually firing a muzzle-loader, with the smell of black gunpowder, the flash of flint on steel and the whistle of lead shot is an all-important part of collecting ancient weapons.

Before embarking on this unique pastime, it is well to follow a few rules and safety measures. All too often folk seem to think that just because a gun is a muzzle-loader, it is not lethal. From all over the world come reports of reckless men blowing themselves (and others) to pieces through all manner of stupid escapades. We learn of rifles being doubled-loaded – for a joke – and of cannoniers losing fingers and hands whilst recharging a smouldering gun barrel. Funny though it may seem, one of the most common injuries is shot-off toes.

Quick-draw clubs are now all the rage in America, Japan and Great Britain. Dressed in full Western rig, our quick-draw fan sports either a Colt or Adams percussion revolver at his side. Each chamber loaded with a measure of powder and a lethal lead ball, he stands facing a full-size 'bad-guy' target. His trigger finger rests lightly on a button set into a wall and, once he reaches for his gun and relieves the pressure on the button, a giant stop-watch will start to time his draw. Speed is of the utmost importance for, not until the lead missile strikes the target, will the ticking clock stop.

Of course, with so much excitement in the air and with cash prizes at stake, it is little wonder that the odd accident occurs. Novices tend to release the button, snatch for their gun and pull the trigger all in one fell swoop. The result is a bullet fired whilst the weapon is still in the holster, straight down into an unsuspecting foot or toe. So many quick-draw fans became members of the Hop-Along Club that it was eventually thought wiser to cast the balls and bullets in beeswax!

Out on the range one can either use a rifle, musket or shotgun. For the rifle, however, one should only use a proper full-bore range; a bullet spinning out of a ·577 Enfield is likely to travel well over 400 yds and still make a mess of a soft target. Smooth-bore muskets or shotguns, whether flint or percussion, are much safer in a limited area, although chances should not be taken with any firearm.

One of the greatest dangers when firing muzzle-loaders lies in discharging a piece with the load not properly rammed home. Leave an air-gap of just half an inch and it will build up enough pressure to blow away part of the breech end. Always ensure that the load is rammed home properly and, with shotguns, make sure a wad rests on top of the load. Another bothersome thing is the blow-back of burnt powder, on which the *Ipswich Journal* of 3 December 1803 has some good advice.

> Hints to Volunteers. . . . In firing, it often happens that some grains of powder are enforced into the face, which may produce great irritation, if not seen attended to. The practise is very simple, and the cure may be affected by anyone. The grains of the powder should be picked out with a needle or toothpick, immediately after the accident; and with a view to prevent inflammation, as well as to dissolve and carry off any particles of the powder that may remain, the parts affected should frequently be washed with warm water; for as the greatest part of gunpowder consists of nitre, a salt very soluble in warm water, it will easily dissolve when it meets with the moisture; and the other two ingredients, sulphur and charcoal, will be washed away at the same time.

Before firing an antique weapon, have a chat with one of the older members of the MLAGB and listen to what he has to say. His experience has been gleaned the hard way – by trial and error. Together with a list of important 'dos and don'ts', he will more than likely set out the following rules of thumb.

1   Make sure that the piece is not loaded. Do this before anything else (see below)!
2   Once the piece is passed safe, then try to strip it down. The lock should be checked over to ensure that all the working parts are safe and sound. Nothing is worse than 'going off at half cock'. If sear or tumbler is worn, have it fixed by a capable gunsmith.
3   With the barrel removed, check this for cracks or deep rust pittings. This applies to the exterior as well as the interior, for hair-line fractures can lie undetected on the underside of the barrel. A good guide is to hang the barrel up by a piece of thin wire or thread attached to the barrel tang. Now strike the barrel gently, using a light hammer or spanner. If the barrel is sound, it will ring like a bell. A duller sound means that all is not well within the metal tube. Although this method is good enough for smooth-bore shotgun or musket, a multi-groove rifle should be X-rayed.
4   Most good quality muzzle-loaders have a removable breech-plug which allows for much closer interior inspection and cleaning. The coarse threading on this plug should be closely inspected for signs of wear and tear and metal fatigue. If the threading looks at all worn, then reassemble your gun and hang it back on the wall as a collector's item only. That plug is all-important and can mean the difference between life and death to the user! The same applies to percussion nipples; if these are not bedded down good and tight, they could blast out into head or eye. It cannot be repeated too often that these old weapons are not toys – they were made to kill and are still capable of so doing.

Once you have established that your gun is in good shooting order, then it is advisable to gather a set of accessories. This will include a powder horn or flask, which should also be inspected to ensure that it is safe and sound as well as being waterproof. A leaking flask makes you very unpopular among other shooters especially if you stand around the firing area! If you are using a muzzle-loading shotgun, then you will also need a leather shot-flask. Some sportsmen carry prepared powder and shot in a paper twist, but I tend to think that the sport lacks a little of its colour and ancient romance if one resorts to this method. What better sight is there than the flash of burnished copper and brass on a cold, crisp, winter's morning as powder and shot go tumbling down a fine old browned barrel!

Next you will need a wad-punch and bullet mould, a set for each size of gun, for the odds on finding two guns with the same bore size are minute. A set of spare nipples, a tin of copper percussion caps, a selection of flints if you are firing a flintlock, and a set of cleaning rods will complete your kit. Gunpowder can only be purchased on permit so a trip to the local police station *before* you buy a shooter would be advisable.

Although it may be easy enough to purchase the antique gun, buying all the odds and ends that go to make up the muzzle loader's kit is a different story. It is a good idea to purchase a copy of the *Guns Review*, a magazine devoted entirely to the wants of the gun-bug. Here you will find lists of firms who specialise in catering to the gun trade. However, it seems to me much easier and far better to join one of the many branches of the MLAGB and take advantage of the free trade that goes on within such bands of collectors and shooters.

Casting your own lead balls is something that is an absolute must. For a Brown Bess or Enfield musket, the ball must be cast true, for any odd air pockets or lumps or bumps could affect the true flight of the missile. To obtain such perfection, one has to know how to get the hot lead to flow without bubbling, and possess a pair of bullet moulds that are free from imperfections. Practice plays an important part in this but a few hints will not come amiss.

First you will need a metal ladle very much along the lines of a soup ladle and large enough to take about half a pound of lead. Mount this ladle and its contents over a fairly high flame, keeping the whole thing on the move until the metal becomes molten. As the lead starts to become fluid, you will find a thin skin of caked muck rising to the surface. This must be removed with the aid of an old spoon, for, if any of this residue finds its way into the mould, the bullet or ball could be affected. Once the skin has been removed, a small knob of beeswax about the size of a pea should be dropped in. This aids the final flow and also burns out any foreign bodies present in the mixture. The act of pouring should be a single, even movement. Pour until the lead rises to the top of the vent on the mould, then, waiting a few seconds for the lead to set, spring open the handles of the mould and drop the missile into a bucket of cold water. Carry on like this until you have the number of balls you require. It is advisable, however, to let the mould cool down from time to time as it can become distorted with the heat. Once the balls have been cast, the next job will be to cut off the sprue-stem, the small piece of lead which projects through the pouring hole after each ball has been cast. On most pincer moulds, there is a pair of cutters for just this purpose and, after the removal of the stem, a light tap with the head of the mould should ensure a perfect sphere. On no account should this task be hurried. Too much vigour in hammering out the imperfection may well result in an elliptical ball. To round off the exercise, roll each ball or bullet in some plumber's tallow (although goose grease or mountain-bear fat should be the order of the day). This makes for easier loading and helps reduce fouling of the barrel, especially in the case of a rifle with heavy bands.

Those who think that firing a muzzle-loader is a simple operation would do well to reflect on the instructions in a military manual of 1672, which gave a step-by-step guide on loading to cavalry units.

All the carabines being dropt (let fall) and hanging by their swivells; the postures are as followeth.
Silence being commanded.
1 Handle your carabine.
2 Mount your carabine, placing your butt end upon your thigh.
3 Rest your carabine in your bridle hand.
4 Bend your cock, to half bent.
5 Guard your cock (slip on the safety dog-catch).
6 Prime your pan.
7 Shut your pan.
8 Sink your carabine on your left side.
9 Gage your flask.
10 Lade your carabine.
11 Draw forth your scouring stick (ramrod).
12 Shorten your scouring stick.
13 Lade with bullet and ramm home.
14 Withdraw your scouring stick.
15 Return your scouring stick.
16 Recover and rest your carabine in your bridle hand.
17 Fix your hammer.
18 Free your cock (slip off safety dog-catch).
19 Present your carabine. (In presenting of the carabine he must rest it upon his bridle arm, placing the butt end to the right side near the shoulder; or at length with his right hand).

20   Give fire. (Note; that the carabine is to be fired about twelve foot distance, and to be levelled at the knees of your enemie's horse, because that by the strength of the powder and motion of the horse your shot may be at random.

21   Drop your carabine.

These postures may serve for the harquebuz; but observe, when at any time you make your approaches towards an enemy, your carabine is to be mounted, with the butt end on your thigh, with your hand above the lock; and so (also) when you march through any town or city; otherwise it may be dropt.

After this brief savour of the past in action to give you a feel for this particular type of militaria, it is as well to know something about the different kinds of weapons which can be collected and the sequence of their development.

MATCHLOCK

This is one of the earliest forms of firepower, utilising a slow-match. This piece of smouldering cord or match was clamped between the jaws of an arm called a serpentine. Once the order 'Fire' or 'Shoot' was given, a lever or trigger was operated which in turn lowered the serpentine into the small pan of priming powder. This powder communicated with the main charge through a tiny vent let into the side of the barrel. The priming powder, once afire, set off the main charge and sent the heavy lead ball whistling and spinning towards its target. Used effectively in most of the major early European wars, the matchlock reached its zenith during the English Civil War. Visitors to the ancient garrison town of Colchester can still see the effect of these weapons when inspecting the peppered timbers of the Ancient Siege House, East Hill. Here the beams have red-ringed markers nailed around the holes where balls hit the building during the famous siege of Colchester in 1648. Although matchlocks of European manufacture command high prices, those of Eastern origin or design can be found for well under £25.

WHEEL-LOCK

A most desirable weapon and one that could be classed as the Rolls-Royce of the antique gun world. Usually made only for the wealthy and élite, the mechanism was a complicated but ingenious piece of engineering. Built very much like an early cigarette lighter of the flint and wheel type, the serrated, hardened steel wheel was 'spanned', i.e. the spindle mounted in the centre of the lock was wound up with a spanner or key, thereby lightening the chain attached to a heavy mainspring which was compressed by the action. The dog-head bearing a piece of iron pyrites in its jaws, lowered down on to the roughened surface of the wheel. When the trigger was engaged, the wheel spun and the fire-stone danced, sending a shower of hot sparks into the pan of priming powder. Wheel-locks, because of their originally high cost, have kept their prices throughout the years. They are, moreover, a rare find, so be prepared to mortgage the house or sell your wife into a harem!

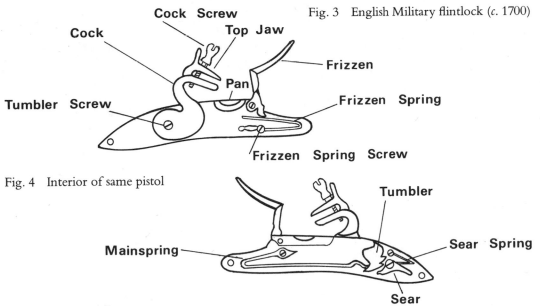

Fig. 3   English Military flintlock (*c.* 1700)

Cock Screw

Cock

Top Jaw

Frizzen

Pan

Tumbler Screw

Frizzen Spring

Frizzen Spring Screw

Fig. 4   Interior of same pistol

Tumbler

Sear Spring

Mainspring

Sear

SNAPHAUNCE

Thought to have originated in Holland during the mid-sixteenth century, the snaphaunce derived its name from the way it snapped forward in the manner of a pecking hen or a 'schnapp-hahn', as the Dutch called it. This, the earliest form of flintlock, can be found in several guises; Scandinavian, Italian and Scottish, as well as Dutch. The pan cover slid back very much in the same manner as that of a wheel-lock, while the steel was mounted on a V-shaped spring which allowed it to be moved backwards and forwards. By far the most popular of the various types was the Dutch snaphaunce which held sway in Africa and India right up to the late 1890s.

FLINTLOCK

The first reference to this form of firepower can be found in 1683, in Turner's *Pallas Armata*. Briefly, it would appear that from the snaphaunce, with its long, awkward steel so prone to damage, there evolved the true flintlock. The sliding pan was incorporated into the L-shaped pan cover with the tempered surface serving as the steel. The cock became that much more elegant over the years while the heavy, banana-shaped lock gave way to the slim, elegant examples to be found on weapons of George IV's reign.

PERCUSSION (Cap-and-ball)

Here then, we come to the end of the true antique firearm. For over two hundred years, the flintlock, in one form or the other, had held sway. With its 'hang-fires',

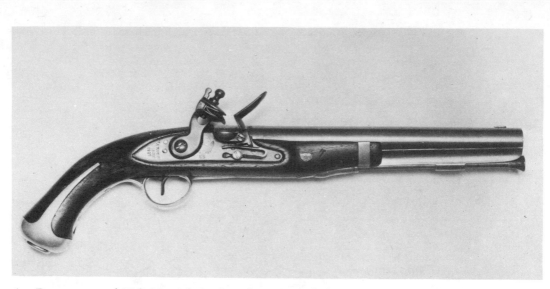

4.   Brass-mounted U.S. Martial pistol made at Harper's Ferry, 1807–8, ·54 calibre, smooth bore

5.   U.S. Martial pistol made by H. Aston & Co. Bought by the U.S. Navy, it is one of only 3,000 marked with anchor and date on tang and barrel

'flash-in-the-pans', 'off-at-half-cocks' and a dozen or more other defects, it had coughed, spluttered, and belched ball, shot, flame and soot all around the discovered world. Men had perished in their thousands on scores of battlefields from the effects of that tiny piece of Brandon flint striking steel. Now, in the year 1840, when the Royal Ordnance started to replace its flintlocks with percussion-cap muskets and pistols, we were to see a system that, within just twenty years, would lead to obsolescence of the muzzle-loader and the introduction of a breech-loading, centre and rim fire cartridge. The recognised inventor of the percussion method was one

Alexander John Forsyth, a minister from Belhelvie, Aberdeenshire, who, in 1807, perfected his 'scent-bottle' lock. This lock, which sported a magazine of fulminate in the shape of a scent bottle, could be so operated as to discharge a small measure of powder which in turn was detonated by the falling hammer. Later, the fulminate was to be housed in a small container, initially of iron and subsequently of copper, which even today is still being used by muzzle-loaders.

Off-shoots of the percussion-lock system are far too numerous to list here, but one should beware of anything that has been altered or adapted.

The law on collecting firearms is all rather strange and complicated to say the least. Up until the 1960s, a rough guide was, 'If it's over a hundred years old, then it's an antique and you can collect it without a licence or permit.' That was alright until the late 1960s; by this ruling, weapons that could be identified as being 1860–70 could also be collected. *But*, as any first-year police cadet could tell you, by then the breech-loader was well under way. Such models as the Martini-Henry, Sharps, Winchester, Gras, Chassepot and a host of other certifiable weapons all rapidly gained popularity in a gun-hungry world. They could not be classed as antique pieces for, with a little ingenuity and a box of World War 1 or 2 cartridges, those folk who were interested could have themselves a real and lethal firearm. Consequently, the rules governing antique weapons were tightened up, although, even now, the rules differ from county to county. However, a fair yardstick would be as follows.

1 If your gun or pistol is a muzzle-loader – that's to say it cannot be broken or opened at the breech to take a cartridge – then you can collect.

2 Percussion cap-and-ball revolvers (and this includes those known as pepper-boxes), can also be collected even if they are still in their original wooden case complete with powder flask, balls and tin of percussion caps. Incidentally, if at any time you hear of a neighbour left with a cased pistol or revolver, try to dissuade them from taking it along to the local police station. I have heard of numerous cases where a poor old dear left all on their own, finding such a weapon, panics because a sticky-beak friend tells them that they'll end up in the Tower for being in possession of a firearm. They rush off to the local police-station and sign over two or three hundred

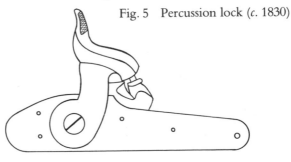

Fig. 5 Percussion lock (*c.* 1830)

23

pounds' worth of gun to the Law. Most police officers would in fact advise her where to take such a valuable piece to sell, once they had satisfied themselves that the piece in question was an antique. However, to make positively sure of status and value, it would be as well to take the advice of a gun expert before signing anything.

3 *You cannot collect without a certificate if you wish to fire the gun in question.* No matter how old it may be, and whether it is a matchlock, wheel-lock, snaphaunce, flintlock or a cap-and-ball percussion piece, if you wish to fire the weapon either for target or sporting events, you must have it on ticket. A visit to your nearest police headquarters *before* you start will save a great deal of bother. Tell them exactly what you aim to use – where, when, and why. Also remember that it is an offence under the Firearms Act to purchase, own or have in your possession a gun or pistol that has been copied or reproduced. Very often one will see advertised fine working models of reproduction antique guns, the most popular of these being the Brown Bess, New Land flintlock and Colt revolver. These stem from all over the world, but those reaching our shops seem to originate from Italy, Japan, the USA and the outbacks of Suffolk and the Midlands. Initially they were made to cater for the needs of those members of clubs specialising in muzzle-loading who didn't wish to take the chance of firing the real thing. With prices of the genuine article escalating week by week, it would be foolish to wreck, say, a pistol of 1800 whilst firing it. Furthermore, with metal fatigue and the general wear-and-tear on all working parts, the chances of a gun blowing up in your hands or face is all too real.

Once again I can only stress that, if you are at all in doubt about what you *can* or *cannot* collect, contact a senior police officer in charge of Firearms at your regional police headquarters. He'll soon put you right!

For the collector of British flintlocks, there is a vast range from which to choose. Some collectors prefer blunderbusses sporting a large bore and with brass or steel barrels. These weapons, so popular with highwaymen, gamekeepers and mail-coach guards, were also issued to the Royal Navy where, during Nelson's time, they saw more than a fair share of action up in the topsails. Usually loaded with a measure of swanshot – each ball being about the size of a pea – this charge, at close range, was capable of blowing a man apart. As if this wasn't deterrent enough, one also finds the occasional spring bayonet mounted either on top or beneath the barrel. A rarity to search for is the blunderbuss with a wicked-looking, curved triangle blade fixed to the barrel side. Closely associated with the large, bell-mouthed blunderbuss are the small blunderbuss pistols. These can also be found with barrels of brass or steel and are sometimes equipped with a small vicious spring bayonet. This weapon was usually sported by ship's officers or Bank runners.

Collecting is, of course, entirely a matter of personal choice and taste. Some will prefer to specialise in long arms like muskets, rifles, carbines and fine fowling pieces, while others will favour the smaller hand-guns. There is something to be said for the latter, if only for the saving on valuable room space. There seems to be far greater variety in pistols because of their wider range of usage and users, be it the common whore who concealed a petite pistol in her muff or scarlet garter, or the man of the cloth who sported a small flintlock pistol, built into his prayer book and discharged by means of a ring and cord trigger!

To the novice, bore sizes are all rather confusing, but, if he consults the following guide which lists the calibre in decimals as well as the bore size, he cannot really go wrong. It is important to remember that bore size indicates the number of balls to the pound (e.g. 4 bore= 4 balls to 1lb; 24 bore= 24 balls to 1lb).

Bore Size	Calibre in Decimals	Bore Size	Calibre in Decimals
4	1·052	30	·546
5	·983	31	·532
6	·924	32	·525
7	·884	33	·520
8	·843	34	·515
9	·804	35	·510
10	·786	36	·506
11	·762	37	·501
12	·747	38	·497
13	·734	39	·491
14	·713	40	·488
15	·703	41	·484
16	·662	42	·480
17	·652	43	·476
18	·649	44	·473
19	·643	45	·469
20	·630	46	·466
21	·627	47	·463
22	·622	48	·458
23	·610	49	·456
24	·577	50	·454
25	·571	60	·429
26	·564	62	·420
27	·560	64	·416
28	·557	87	·375
29	·554	100	·323

Among the many marks on a firearm, some of which have already been mentioned, one can often find, stamped into lock or barrel, an odd-looking number,

6. First model LeMat Percussion pistol

such as D.U. 8922 or, in some instances, the name, Dublin Castle. This was, in fact, a procedure introduced under an Irish Arms Act of 1843 when all weapons, both ancient and modern, had to be stamped and recorded. For a great number of years it was wrongly assumed that guns bearing this mark had been issued for use in the castle itself (there are other examples which bear the stamp of forts and castles elsewhere in Ireland).

For those of you wishing to specialise in percussion revolvers there is also a bewildering variety. Of course, a Colt is always desirable although there are a number of British revolvers that would fill the bill admirably, among them, Kerr, Deane, Adams & Deane, Tranter and the famous Webley.

I suppose that Samuel Colt is a name that readily conjures up stories of the Wild West, Gold Rush Days and the American Civil War. Not a few have been found tucked away in Britain – relics of a long-forgotten grandfather who made the journey westwards during the mid-nineteenth century in search of fame and fortune. Returning home, with or without a fortune, his gun was tossed into a shed or attic as casually as a pair of boots would be discarded.

The last cased Colt that I heard of emerging like this was found about three years ago. Out in the rural district of Great Bentley, Essex, are a number of small farms and orchards. In summertime, students who help out with the harvest can also, if they have a mind, search for hidden antiques in old barns, sheds and haylofts. One such chappie, working in an orchard happened to stumble across a derelict shed which, besides holding the usual household and garden debris, also had the remains of a large sideboard jammed inside. Asking permission of the farmer's wife, he started to root about among the odds and ends that were packed inside. Imagine his surprise when he found, just sitting on top of a pile of yellowing newspapers and, wrapped up in a piece of old rag, a small pocket Colt! Imagine his even greater surprise when he also found, scattered at the back of the sideboard, the flask, oil bottle and various tools.

Waiting for the return of the farmer, the student produced his find and asked if the farmer was willing to sell. 'Oh yes!' he said, 'But you'll want that old wooden box to go with it won't you?' It seemed that our farmer's little lad had been playing with this family heirloom among the leafy trees. One day, being called indoors in rather a hurry, he had left the percussion revolver, case and all, out in the orchard. A few days later the farmer, catching sight of the revolver and the accessories lying on the grass, picked them up and, wrapping the firearm in a piece of old oily rag, tossed it and the odds and ends into the back of the sideboard. The case he had forgotten about until the young student had jogged his memory. Wandering off up to the top end of the orchard, farmer and eager youth eventually found the weather-beaten remains of the oak case. Weeks of sodden rain had taken its toll. The case was apart at the seams, the green baize lining all discoloured and adrift and the original Colt label just a piece of pulp! My young friend bought the lot and tried his best to repair the case, but to no avail. Although the gun and accessories fitted the case, when you looked at them set out they just didn't look right. The case seemed to be that much older and more worn than the actual revolver. So, yet another unit of firearm history was to be split up for, as the case gave the appearance of having been 'married', the proud owner decided to discard the battered case and keep the revolver in a leather holster instead. He knew that the case was right, but his gun collecting friends didn't, and wouldn't believe that the set was original – a sad comment on the consequences of child's play.

There are, as has been said, a number of Colts that one can collect, one of the most sought after, for the British collector, being that with the London address.

Starting with those manufactured at Colt's workshop in Paterson, New Jersey from 1836 onwards, we find three general sizes of single-action percussion revolver: Belt, ·36 cal.; Pocket, ·31 cal. (also ·28 cal.); and Holster, a hard kicking ·44 cal. intended primarily for the military market. The heavy, soft lead bullet of this was capable of blasting a charging man out of a saddle or tossing him bodily across a room.

COLT MODELS

PATERSON MODEL	1836–42. Calibres: ·28, ·31, ·34, ·36. Approx. 2,000 manufactured.
WALKER MODEL	1847. Calibre: ·44. Approx. 1,100 manufactured.
DRAGOON-OLD ARMY	1847–62. Calibre: ·44. Approx. 21,000 manufactured, with 700 bearing English markings.

OLD MODEL POCKET	Wells Fargo: 1848; Baby Dragoon: 1847–49. Calibre: ·31. Approx. 11,000 manufactured.
OLD MODEL POCKET 1849	1849–75. Calibre: ·31. Approx. 330,000 manufactured, with 11,000 coming from the London factory in 1853–59.
OLD MODEL NAVY	1850–72 (Navy Belt Model 1851). Calibre: ·36. Approx. 215,000 manufactured with an additional 40,000 from the London factory (1853–57).
NEW MODEL POCKET	1853–72 (Root 1855 Sidehammer). Calibres: ·265, ·28, and ·31. Approx. 40,000 manufactured.
NEW MODEL ARMY	1860–72 (1860 Army Model). Calibre: ·44. Approx. 200,000 manufactured.
NEW MODEL NAVY	1861–72 (1861 Round Barrel Navy). Calibre: ·36. Approx. 38,000 manufactured.
NEW MODEL POLICE	1862–72 (1862 Belt Model). Calibre: ·36. Approx. 25,000 manufactured.

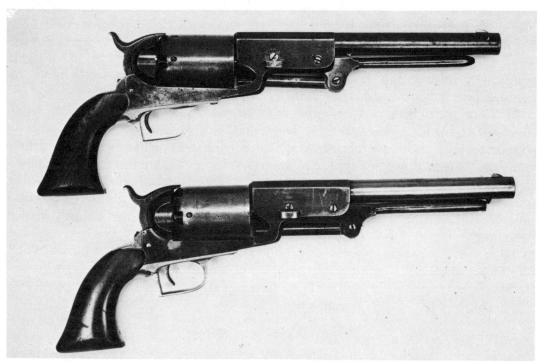

7.   Pair of Colt Model 1847 pistols (dragoon), 6 shot, ·44 calibre, weight 4lb 1oz

When purchasing a Colt of any description, be sure to check it out before parting with your cash. Better still, take that knowledgeable friend along with you for added support. With Colt percussion revolvers fetching a hundred pounds or more, unscrupulous dealers and collectors are not beyond 'doctoring' the odd piece. A number are being built from 'Continental Colts' – a term which covers a multitude of sins – for these copies were churned out in their thousands to be sold to various Middle East powers during the late nineteenth century. Having been scrapped for the past forty to fifty years they have lain rusting in arsenals. They would, I expect, still be there but for the wiles of some enterprising dealer, who, seeing a vast profit to be made, bid for the whole lot – lock, stock and barrel so to speak! Shipped back to Britain by the sackful, this mixture of odds and ends, some whole, some damaged, some rusted together in a solid mass, began to appear on the British market. True, they weren't sold as genuine Colts to begin with, but, after one or two changes of ownership and a little refurbishing, the trade began to suffer a sudden influx of 'Army', 'Navy', and 'Pocket Colts'.

To guard against these rogue revolvers, it is necessary to check all the serial numbers, which are usually to be found on the butt strap, trigger guard, barrel, ramrod and cylinder. Ramrod and cylinder are two of the most usual replacements but something else which has just come to light through the diligent researches of Mr E. Dixon Larson is the phenomenon of 'shortened and stretched barrels'. He reports in the *Arms Gazette* Vol 1, No 5.

'A detailed study was conducted to determine the most commonly misrepresented models. It was concluded that the Colt Rammerless Model, frequently referred to as the 'Wells Fargo', is the faker's number one choice, as it outnumbers all others at a ratio of three to one. Usually a common 1849 Colt Pocket Model is reworked by removing the rammer assembly. Filling in the rammer cradle holes, loading cut-out lug and cropping the barrel to the desired length of 3 inches. The welding and shaping involved in this modification is simple and easily camouflaged by false aging.

'Another "faker's" choice is the transforming of the standard Colt Army Model of 1860 into the Army Model with a fluted cylinder. This is usually accomplished by a skilled machinist who merely cuts flutes in the cylinder of a common model. The patent date in the flute is added by engraving or stamping.'

Mr Dixon Larson goes on to explain how, with the aid of a $(NH4)2S208$ compound, he is able to determine whether a piece has been added, altered, or tampered with by a welding method.

29

FAMOUS GUNSMITHS

Among the most important names to look for when buying an antique firearm are the following.

Robert & James Adams, also *Deane, Adams & Deane,* 30 King William St, London (1851–92).   In 1856 the firm was taken over by the London Armoury Co. Patentee of a fine, solid-frame percussion revolver with double action. Specialising in three types: the Navy ·44 calibre, the Dragoon ·50 calibre and the Pocket ·32 calibre.

W. Brander, Minories, London. (1690–1750); *W. B. Brander,* Minories, London (1750–1825); *Brander & Potts,* 70 Minories, London and Winchelsea (1825–32). Held extensive Government contracts for flintlock pistols and muskets and also made brass-barrel flintlock carbines for East India Company.

Durs Egg of London (1770–1834)   A gunsmith who enjoyed the patronage of the Prince Regent (George IV) and made a flintlock, breech-loading carbine of his own design as well as numerous flintlock rifles, carbines and muskets under Government contract.

Lacy & Co of London (1776–1840), later *Lacy & Reynolds* (1840–53)   Makers of holster pistols and muskets, both flintlock and percussion. Also known for over-and-under and side-by-side double-barrel percussion pistols. Worked under Government contract and also for East India Company.

John Manton, 6 Dover Street, London (1780–1820)   The elder of two brothers who became world-famous for their guns. Made heavy-bore hunting rifles and flintlock, swivel wall guns.

Henry Nock of London and Birmingham (1760–1810)   One of the first gunmakers to perfect the sliding safety engaged behind the cock or hammer. Also made four- and seven-barrel flintlock guns. His weapons were extensively carried and used by all ranks and are to be found the world over.

William Tranter, Birmingham and London (1853–5)   Famous for his percussion revolvers with two triggers. Made weapons under Government contract for both percussion and metallic rim fire cartridge revolvers.

T. Twigg, London (1760–80); *Twigg & Bass* (1780–3); then reverted to *Twigg* (1783–1813)   Specialised in officers' flintlock pistols, multi-shot and pepper-box-type flintlock pistols, as well as pistols bearing spring bayonets and concealed daggers.

John Witton of London (1840–9), later *Witton & Daw,* 82 Bond Street and 57 Threadneedle Street, London (1849–78)   Specialised in naval weapons, makers of naval percussion pistols with belt hooks, under Government contract.

Wogdon (1760–97), at premises in London and Dublin; later *Wogdon & Barton* (1797–1820)   Makers of fine flintlock holster pistols and carbines under Government contract.

30

OTHER LEADING GUNSMITHS

Patrick Ferguson (1774–1780)   Born at Pitfour, Scotland in 1744, he joined the Royal North British Dragoons at the tender age of 14 and saw action in Germany. Never of very robust health, he eventually obtained a captaincy in the 70th Regiment serving in Tobago, but due to further illness returned to his native Scotland where he invented and perfected a flintlock, breech-loading rifle. This he demonstrated before a commission of the Master-General of Ordnance at Woolwich on 1 June 1776. So successful was the rifle that the authorities ordered one hundred rifles complete with bayonets, this being made under Government contract by Durs Egg and Ezekiel Baker. After a suitable training period, Ferguson and a company of men embarked for service in America where they saw action at the Battle of Brandywine. Although severely wounded during this battle, Ferguson was to partake in a number of skirmishes until 7 October 1780. On that day he fought his last battle on top of King's Mountain, South Carolina, where he was killed together with a great number of his men.

The Ferguson Rifle, one of the most sophisticated forms of early breech-loader, owed its success to the number of channels cut in the screw-plug. These alleviated the jamming found in earlier breech-loaders. His rifle saw service with troops of the East India Company and volunteer militia forces, and is very much sought after today *if found in original military issue condition*. A Ferguson Patent sporting rifle also proved very popular during the eighteenth century and was manufactured by S. Turner and Wilson of London, F. Innis of Edinburgh, and Newton of Grantham.

T. W. Field (1750–1790)   Made fine screw or turn-off brass-barrel flintlock pistols. Had a shop at Aylesbury, Buckinghamshire.

Harman Barne (1635–70)   Was a gunmaker to royalty – among his many élite clients was Prince Rupert. Made one of the earliest known breech-loading flintlock rifles which saw service during the Civil War. Had a shop in London and marked his pieces 'Londini'.

W. R. Pape (1865–90)   A gunsmith who did much to develop and patent the chokebore shotgun. Also worked on early metallic cartridges. Several examples of his work can be seen in the Museum of Science & Engineering, Newcastle-upon-Tyne. Had a shop at Newcastle-upon-Tyne.

W. Parker (c. 1840)   Specialised in making weapons for the East India Company, especially cased travelling percussion pistols for officers. Had a shop in London.

Charles Pickfatt (1660–1750, a two generation firm)   Famous for his screw or turn-off barrel flintlock holster pistols boasting silver mask butt-caps and wire inlay. Had a shop in London.

T. H. Potts (1840–53)   Was under Government contract to make the famous Brunswick percussion rifle, the first percussion weapon to be used by the British Services. Made percussion pocket pistols with detachable daggers. Also brass barrel naval percussion pistols and finely engraved presentation pieces. Had a shop at Haydon Square, London. In 1853 the name changed to Potts & Hunt.

James Purdey (1816–68)   Famous firm of gunsmiths with a shop at 314 Oxford Street, London. Made percussion pocket pistols, double-barrel percussion shotguns and rifles. 'Purdey' flintlock fowling pieces being top of a collector's list. In 1868 the name changed to *James Purdey & Sons*, the business being transferred to Audley House, South Audley Street, London.

John Rigby (1867–90)   Made double-barrel, over-and-under percussion pistols, sporting belt hooks and bell muzzle, brass-barrel percussion pistols. Shops in London and Dublin. Name changed to *John Rigby & Co Ltd,* at 43 Sackville Street, London, with a factory at 5 Crown Yard, Stanhope Street, London (1890–1900).

Segalas or Segallas (1721–1800)   A rather ornate type of flintlock pocket pistol, bearing the forged word 'A Londres' or 'London' on the barrel or lock. Although highly ornamental the workmanship was inferior and lacking in quality. They were mostly manufactured in Belgium or France.

Samuel & Charles Smith (1849–75)   Specialised in officers' holster pistols with pill-lock mechanism, also double-barrel, percussion sporting guns. Shop at 64 Princes Street, Leicester Square, London.

S. Staudenmayer (1790–1830)   Famous for his double-barrel, over-and-under flintlock pocket pistols. Had a shop in London.

Tipping and Lawden (1840–77)   Worked on Government contracts for naval percussion pistols, also produced the small, four-barrel cartridge pistols on the Sharps (USA) Patent. Had a shop in Birmingham.

Unwin & Rodgers (c. 1850)   Famous for their percussion combination pistol and knife. The huge blade was mounted along the barrel. Had a shop at Sheffield.

Utting (1800–20)   Made coaching blunderbusses and double-barrel boxlock, flintlock pocket pistols. Had a shop in Birmingham.

John Waters (1767–81)   Fine quality weapons from this gunsmith who made brass-barrel flintlock pistols. Famous for a brass, cannon-barrel flintlock coaching pistol with a patent spring bayonet. Had a shop at Birmingham.

Once the nucleus of a collection has been started, the next logical and important considerations are cleaning, preservation and method of display.

Nothing is more annoying to a gun/sword/dagger/bayonet or medal collector than visitors who want to handle his exhibits. To many non-collectors, his most treasured items are nothing more than toys and, just like toys, are there to be played with. Time and time again, I hear of fully grown men playing cowboys or highwaymen and dry-firing old flinters or percussion revolvers with disastrous effects – shattered cocks and hammers, chipped sears and nipples, or even part of a stock fracturing where a main-spring has broken under stress and forced its way through the woodwork. If you *must* try the cocking mechanism, do so carefully and gently. Ensure that, when releasing the trigger and hammer, a strong thumb restrains the moving parts. By this means, if the second engagement is worn or unstable, the piece cannot then fly off at half cock causing unnecessary damage.

A strong word of warning to everyone handling firearms of any age, be they antique or early breech-loaders. *Make sure the piece is not loaded.* One of the oldest known cries must surely be, 'We didn't know the gun was loaded!'

With an antique weapon, the easiest way to ascertain if a charge still slumbers deep in the breech, is to find a long, thin, but firm stick or rod. Ram this down the barrel as far as it will go and mark it level with the muzzle. Remove the rod and lay it against the outside of the barrel from touch-hole or nipple to muzzle. If it protrudes by about half an inch then beware, for there could be some form of load down there. If you think this sounds rather over-cautious, then ponder on this tale:

A number of years ago, I tracked down a pair of small flintlock pocket pistols by Archer of London. For years they had served as hat-pegs on a rather ornate hall stand. Jammed on dowel rods and turned upside down, they really served their purpose very well. Finally I managed to buy them and took them home. A friend of my wife picked up one of the pistols and, before anyone could stop her, presented it to her left breast and pulled the trigger. She did this a couple of times before I managed to snatch the weapon from her hand. Next morning I took the pistols into the workshop and turned-off both barrels. There, in both chambers, was not only gunpowder, but brown paper patches and tiny, but deadly, lead balls! Taking a pinch of powder from each charge, I set up a tray to establish just how active it really was. Sure enough, with a slight puff and a flash, both little piles took fire immediately they were touched off. Luckily for our playful friend the pistols had, with countless years of wax polishing, received an overall protective coating of polish which had filled the vents and pans and so saved her life.

Damage to pieces, is not, however, only caused by rough handling. As many collectors know from bitter experience, a number of folk suffer from 'poison fingers'. Coin and medal collectors live in absolute dread of that visitor who pounces on their prime pieces, leaving sets of sweaty fingerprints all over the surfaces. It is not so bad for a weapon collector *if* he catches the culprits sweaty-handed, as it were. With the aid of a silicon cloth, he can manage to erase the acid marks. However, for a coin or medal man, fingerprints can cause damage and destruction which no amount of cleaning can eradicate, and, indeed, cleaning of coins is strictly taboo!

Cleaning is another matter governed largely by taste. One collector may well like to see row upon row of highly burnished pieces, while others like to exhibit their weapons just as they were found. However, there should be something of a happy medium. Much damage is admittedly caused by the over-enthusiastic manipulation of a power-drill with whirring wire brushes and lamb's-wool mops, but, equally, a weapon which is allowed to just sit and gather a coating of rust and dirt does not increase in value or beauty at all.

Before any cleaning is attempted try to establish what the original finish was – burnished, blued or perhaps browned.

Burnished weapons, usually found on Cadet or Volunteer pieces where over-cleaning seems to have been the order of the day, can be kept in pristine condition by the light application of wire-wool and oil. A blued metal finish was, and still is, a skilled method of applying heat and chemicals until the distinctive blue-black finish is obtained. If you do manage to find a percussion revolver with more than half of its original finish, leave it as it is. Despite our progress in other fields, present-day gunsmiths cannot unfortunately seem to capture that true-blue bloom of yore.

Browning, a method of controlled rusting, is to be found on good quality shotguns, pistols and early muskets. Take great care when attempting to clean a barrel or lock which *looks* rusty. That red patina could well be covering up a fine coating of browning. Most famous of all 'browned' pieces must surely be the old 'Brown Bess', a flintlock musket which saw action the world over with the British Army.

There are various stages of cleaning, from the quick wipe-over with an oily cloth, to the complete strip-down. For those who balk at the idea of stripping a weapon down, then the former method will suffice. Now, for those of you who want to strip down lock, barrel and furniture, it is advisable to procure a set of suitable screw-drivers and drifts and an excellent book, *Antique Firearms, Their Care, Repair & Restoration* by Ronald Lisker, pub. Herbert Jenkins. Nothing is worse than handling a fine pistol or musket only to discover the ravages of a do-it-yourself gunsmith who, with the aid of a screwdriver or old kitchen knife, has attempted to overhaul his favourite piece.

Soaking with a Plus-Gaz mixture is good for removing stubborn patches of rust, but, whatever you do, don't rush the process – soak, leave, inspect and try to remove the offending patch with the aid of wire-wool, then soak and leave again. Remember, it has taken something like a hundred years for that rust to build up, so take it easy when trying to remove it. Clean out all the loose dirt from inside the lock and barrel areas but, once again, be careful not to scratch or mark the woodwork. Once it is clean and dry, give all the wood a liberal coating of boiled linseed, using the palm of the hand to massage it in thoroughly. Time and gentle effort expended here will be rewarded by the warm antique glow that the stock eventually takes on. Once the weapon has been reassembled, it is advisable to give the whole piece, both metal and wood, a wipe-over with a good-quality wax polish to give added protection.

In these days of box-like housing, with rooms designed to take only the odd human being or two, displaying a collection can prove something of a problem. Wall mounting can produce a good effect, provided that the wall will take the weight. Far better from all aspects is the gun cabinet which, built like a large china-display cabinet, can stand against a wall and house a fair selection of guns. For those with limited funds or space, it is possible to adapt an old sideboard or dresser by setting out pistols and revolvers on shelves or trays.

Whichever method you favour, don't forget to get the collection well insured. You may think that the pieces you own are not really worth insuring, but, remember, that gun which cost only a tenner five years ago has more than likely risen to ten times that amount. If you are leaving your house unattended for a day or two, it is equally important to deposit your valuables at the nearest bank vault. Failing that, notify the local police station of your absence.

POWDER AND SHOT FLASKS

Closely associated with antique firearms are the rather ornate powder and shot flasks. These can be found in all shapes and sizes, ranging from the petite priming flask to the large hunting flask carried by deer or duck hunters.

By far the most popular are the early nineteenth century examples of copper and brass. There are over 1,500 different patterns to choose from, and the flasks were largely manufactured by such firms as Hawksley, Sykes, Dixon, and the French firm of Bosche. Further information on flasks can be found in the fine work of Ray Riling, *The Powder Flask Book*. For those who set their sights on much earlier examples, it is possible to find flasks of wood, boiled horn, leather, ormolu, antler, silver niello, ivory and tortoiseshell which date back to the sixteenth century.

Flasks with East India Company or American colonial origins often carry small vignettes scratched or scrimshawed over the horn detailing either a date, regimental details or historical events. These are highly desirable and command quite a high price when in original condition. Strange as it may seem, it is still possible to find these horns tucked away among the rubbish of out-the-way junk shops; the base and banjo-plug sometimes get lost, leaving the piece looking like a battered old hunting horn. If you are lucky enough to find such a relic, take a close look around the base and nozzle end for traces of nail or pin holes. These will confirm that the horn you are holding was indeed a powder flask.

High on our list are the American flasks which accompanied the Colt revolver or the popular New England flintlock pistol. These carried a number of designs, the most famous being a 'Stand of Arms' and 'Clasped Hands'. Shop carefully though. There are reproductions on the market. These, in themselves, are not so bad but a few have fallen into the hands of the fakers who are aging them and passing them off as the genuine article. The best way to check on these is to take off the nozzle cap (usually held in place with three grub-screws), and peer down inside the flask. Traces of aging fluid and new solder as well as the crisp sharpness of six-month-old thread marks will tell you all.

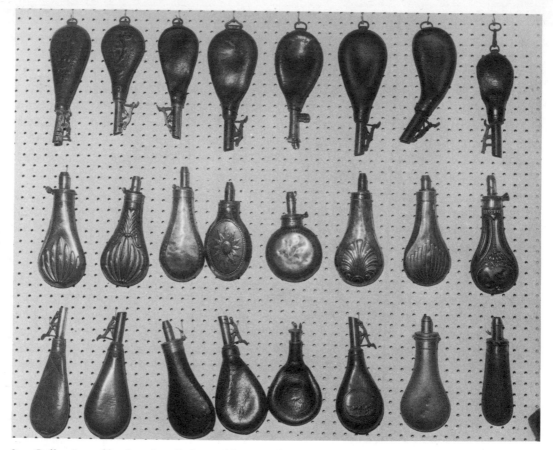

8. Collection of leather shot flasks, and brass and copper gunpowder flasks

If you are going to collect flasks, you will want a good selection of shot flasks. These, like the powder flask, come in various designs and were made by the same firms. They are to be found in pigskin, hide, calf and a thin leather glued to a shaped, tin shell.

Once again, the cleaning of these flasks is all a matter of taste. However, the copper and brass ones look well polished, while the shot flasks respond well to a dressing of saddle-soap or leather-polish. A word of warning – if you are lucky enough to find a mint, virgin flask with its original coating of shellac, don't try cleaning this off. They are rather rare in this condition and are consequently much sought after.

2 Imperial German and Nazi Regalia

Over the past few years, great interest has been shown in the military regalia of our former formidable enemy, Germany. Basically, this interest is divided between items of the old Imperial era and those of Hitler's Nazi Party. The trappings and regalia of these epochs which, for years, have slumbered forgotten in garages, outhouses and lofts, are now being searched for by collector and dealer alike. Spoils from two world wars, in the form of bayonets, helmets, flags, epaulettes and even less martial items like Nazi knives, forks and platters all have a value and a premium to the collector of militaria.

HEADGEAR

Among the most interesting pieces of military equipment that a novice can collect are the various hats and helmets of both periods. However, careful research is necessary to find and correctly identify 'tween the wars stuff. During the Weimar Republic and early Nazi days (1919–28), a mass of World War 1 headgear was utilised for both military and political purposes.

Strange as it may seem, most headgear worn during World War 1 can be found in far better condition than its World War 2 counterpart. *Pickelhauben*, made from jacked or boiled leather with brass or white metal mounts are very hard-wearing and take a lot of knocking about. Remember, too, that nearly every returning Tommy brought with him a 'Kaiser Bill' helmet for his kids to kick about or to stand in pride of place on the sideboard. In view of the lapse of time, the number which still survive after all these years is most surprising. One of the most sought-after of these helmets is that of the Prussian *Garde du Corps*, which reflects the full majesty of the militant Prussian, with its highly polished brass dome and proud silver-gilt parade eagle. Prices for these have soared in the last few years; a far from mint example changed hands at an auction sale in late 1973 for £670 ($1,400). Another favoured piece is the impressive helmet worn by 'other ranks' of the Saxony *Garde Reiter*.

The *Pickelhaube* (literally 'spiked helmet'), was first introduced into the Prussian Army in 1842. The long spike originally represented a spearhead. In 1846, Prussian

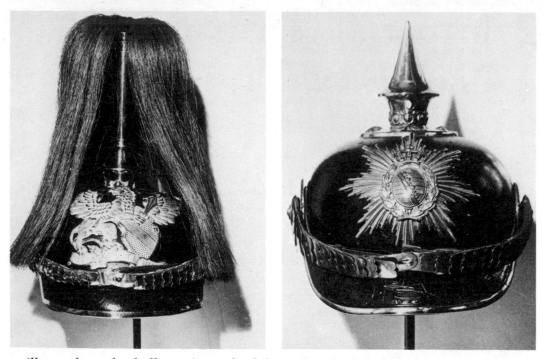

artillery adopted a ball-top instead of the spike on their helmets, to symbolize a cannon-ball. On some early patterns the spike can be removed from its bayonet-fitting mount to reveal a serrated metal knob. Before the hand grenade became a sophisticated weapon, it had to be fused by lighting the length of slow-match protruding from the head. In inclement conditions, this could prove somewhat dangerous, so the problem was resolved by incorporating the fuse into a safety match which could be lit by being scraped across a rough surface – the serrated knob. A painting by Fritz Erler well illustrates the type of slow-match that German infantrymen carried in their teeth before the introduction of the 'safety match'.

On Prussian helmets there is a single state cockade – of black-white-black worn on the right. The left side is unadorned with this metal disc. Following the conclusion of the 1870–71 Franco–Prussian War, the German Empire was founded on 18 January 1871 by William I, King of Prussia, who became the first German Emperor. A cockade bearing the Imperial German colours (red, white and black), was now worn on the right side of the helmet, while the State cockade was sported on the left.

The *Pickelhaube* was worn well into World War 1, with various types being made from felt, tin or even heavy cardboard. It finally gave way to the now familiar steel helmet which was to prove one of the finest pieces of protective headgear of this century. Not only did it stand up to flying shrapnel, but the large brim and nape

9.   *Opposite left:* Band-master's *pickelhaube* of 1st Baden Bodyguard Dragoons, *c.* 1900. The plumes are red horsehair

10.   *Opposite right:* Officer's helmet of 101st Infantry Regiment, Emperor William, King of Prussia's Grenadiers – 2nd Saxon, *c.* 1900

11.   *Above left:* Fine example of trooper's parade helmet, Prussian *Garde du Corps, c.* 1900

12.   *Above right:* World War I Bavarian *ersatz* pressed tin 'other ranks' helmet

13.   *Right:* 1915 pattern mounted rifleman's (*jager zu pferde*) helmet (other ranks)

protected the wearer from the foul weather encountered in the trenches.

Preserving the highly polished finish of a *Pickelhaube* means a comprehensive cleaning operation. First strip off all the mounts, the badge, cockades and chinstrap. Make sure that these are safely packed away. To discover at the end of a cleaning session that one of the studs or screws has gone missing is, to say the least, frustrating. Then, using a piece of flannel, rub shoe polish mixed with a little methylated spirit into the nude leather skull, with a small circular motion of the hand – what is called in the Guards and RMP, 'bulling with small circles'. Continue this process for about thirty minutes then finish off the helmet with a clean, soft duster. All this elbow grease will go much further if the *Pickelhaube* is kept out of direct sunlight, which will fade the polished surface.

Although many cheap and shoddy reproductions are being sold and passed off as the genuine article, it is not difficult to distinguish between the real item and the copy. However, leading sale rooms and collectors now realise that helmets sans mounts, badge or chinstrap are being refitted with reproduction parts. Cockades, in the form of a thin, stamped metal disc painted in the State or national colours, are also being made in the Midlands and fitted to genuine helmets. It is not all that hard to distinguish between the reproduction and the genuine article provided one has the two examples to compare. Paint is yet another important factor; the colour and texture of a fake will be far too bright for an article which has supposedly lain in store for over fifty years.

Prone though they are to damage by dust, damp and moth, cloth hats and caps do still pop up from time to time. They nearly always bear signs of their long years of hibernation. Mitre caps (*c.* 1715), have found their way into British and American collections after being 'liberated' from museums in Germany during World War 2, but many are late nineteenth-century copies made for pageants or important military tattoos. Discretion should be exercised if you contemplate purchasing one of these mitre caps. You could be tempted into paying a high price for a supposedly genuine article – some copies are so good that only an expert could expose them.

Of particular interest to collectors are the officers' caps of 1914–18 period. These have a very small peak and two miniature cockades mounted on the front; the Imperial German cockade of red, white and black above and the State cockade below. Other ranks' caps from this period also survive. Although built along the same lines, they do not have a peak and are slightly inferior in material and finish. Headgear from the inter-war period often displayed three badges – the national emblem (eagle and swastika), the Reich cockade and, in between these, a memorial badge, which was worn to identify the wearers with old Prussian regiments.

When collecting steel helmets which are without insignia, do remember that World War 1 helmets can always be distinguished by the pair of horn-like projections surmounted on either side of the brim. These were originally intended for a heavy steel visor – part of the heavy body armour issued to snipers in forward positions. Although deemed necessary at the time, it proved too cumbersome to be practical and was discarded shortly after its introduction. A complete suit is now something of a rarity and much sought after by the collector. An example will fetch quite a high price on the open market.

Helmets worn by *SS* divisions are also something of a speciality. There is considerable variety in their decoration, from hand-painted insignia to the various transfers found on at least four different types of *SS* helmets. Particularly interesting are those bearing the insignia of the *SS* Officers' School, Tölz, and of the Shalborg Corps or 'Germanische *SS* Dänemark', as a study of *Uniforms of the SS*, Vol 2, (Germanische-*SS* 1940–45)' by Hugh Page Taylor will show. Some of the early *SS* helmets do in fact bear horns of the World War 1 type, and should be carefully inspected to ensure that they carry the correct stamp marks.

Helmets worn by the *Wehrmacht* sported a hunched eagle and swastika on the left side with the national colours on the right. Very similar in design was the navy or *Kriegsmarine* helmet, though this had the slight variation of having a gold eagle. *Luftshutze* (ARP/Civil Defence) personnel had a winged wreath and anti-aircraft gun insignia on the front of their helmets, while the Luftwaffe wore the swooping eagle and swastika on the left side and the national colours on the right. A clip-on camouflage cover was also generally issued. This had summer foliage on one side and rusty, autumn colouring on the other. On the Russian front with its terrible winter conditions, a rather unique form of camouflage face-netting was introduced. Such camouflage helmets are now quite rare and, when found in good condition, command a high price.

During the latter part of World War 2, steel became a scarce commodity and helmets were made of nothing more than thin tin, rather like the helmets worn by miners or oil-riggers today. Helmets of the National Socialist Vehicle Corps (NSKK), were rather elaborate leather creations which were often worn for riots or parades and had an alloy badge depicting a large eagle and wreath on the front. In action, the regulation steel helmet was worn with the appropriate transfer badges. Parachute troops wore a steel helmet of special design with a shock-proof chin strap and the Luftwaffe insignia on the left side, while, for the early part of the war, the Panzer Korps sported a black beret with a reinforced lining. This was later replaced by the conventional *Stahlhelme*.

Although not strictly a military organisation, the Hitler Youth (*Hitler-Jugend* or HJ), was formed to give basic military grounding to thousands of German youngsters. It covered all branches of the fighting forces and, by the time a lad had reached eighteen he was familiar with most of the problems that he would encounter when he joined the Services. This training was put to good use in the latter stages of World

War 2, when the Hitler-Jugend helped to load and service anti-aircraft guns, man anti-tank weapons and slip stick-grenades between the tracks of Russian tanks. Their helmets and hats carry a diamond-shaped badge, bearing the national colours and the Nazi emblem in the centre. Young people were grouped into the various formations and organisations as follows: *Deutchesjungvolk* (DJV), lads between ten and fourteen: *Hitler-Jugend* (HJ), lads between fourteen and eighteen; *Jungmädel*, girls between ten and fourteen years; *Bunddeutschermädel* (BdM), girls between fourteen and eighteen years.

For the collector of headgear from the Nazi period, the scope is exceptionally vast and complicated. Members of the Party organisation wore numerous types of cap, hat and kepi from its very beginning in 1923, with changes taking place right up to the final defeat in 1945. A collector thus has little hope of acquiring or, indeed, identifying all of them, but should at least be aware of the range that exists.

First and foremost, we have the familiar kepi of the SA or Brownshirt divisions which later gave way to the *SS* units. The *SS* peaked cap is readily identified by the small black-and-white label sewn inside, bearing the official stamp and number. A typical example might read: '*SS Dienstmutze. Unbefugter Besitz parteiamtlicher Kleidungsstücke wird laut Verordnung des Reichspräsidenten von 21.3.1933 mit Gefängnis bis zu 2 Jahren bestraft. NSDAP Reichszeugmeisterei Nr 0000*; or, more comprehensibly, '*SS* Service cap. Unauthorised possession of official Party clothing is punishable with imprisonment of up to two years by the Reich-president's decree of 21.3.1933. Party Master of the Ordnance No 0000.' The same label was used in the side-cap (cf. British 'forage cap'), but this reads '*SS Feldmütze*' (*SS* field service cap), instead of '*SS Dienstmütze*'.

It is wise to check round the edges of this label for signs of fresh sewing, as many post-war caps are being doctored and passed off as Nazi items. Yet another clue is the diamond-shaped section found in the crown of the hat; this is a grease-proof compartment in which the owner could display his name, number and regiment. Pre-1945 caps had this section covered in celluloid, whereas the post-war cap has a plastic covering. This detail may seem rather petty, but when a genuine *SS* cap can change hands for around £35 ($65–$70) and a very similar post-war taxi-driver's cap for a couple of pounds ($4), it pays to be careful. Among the bewildering variety of other caps worn by members of the *SS* are the fez, a kepi, a field-grey, peakless cap and a fur cap worn on the Russian Front.

UNIFORMS
Uniforms of the Imperial German Army are still obtainable, but, unless they have been in a private collection, they do tend to be the worse for wear. Nothing can really rectify the damage inflicted by moths, and to have the holes repaired is a long and expensive operation. If you do have the good fortune to obtain Imperial German tunics, ensure that they are well protected with an anti-moth spray and kept out of direct sunlight. Better still, invest in a transparent plastic cover for each item.

The early Nazi period produced uniforms that were a mixture of World War 1 service and sporting wear, well covered with party insignia. Any of the early photographs of Hitler and Hess addressing their men well illustrate this improvisation. It was not until 1929 that the brown, SA uniform became standard and well into 1936 before the black uniform of the *SS* was universally adopted. One rumoured reason for the popularity of the brown shirts was that the Party managed to purchase, at a knock-down price, thousands of Government-surplus brown shirts. Curiously, the popular myth that the *SS* stormed through Europe dressed in a terrible black uniform still prevails. Terrible though their assault on Russia and Europe was, it was not conducted in black. From 1938, the sombre black was replaced by the field-grey which was to become a familiar sight on battlefields from Stalingrad to Berlin. Its wearers fought so boldly that, out of the 240,000 men listed, only 40,000 could be accounted for in the last year of the war.

A fascinating uniform which has eluded both the student of *SS* military history and the collector is the little-known British *SS* Legion of St George. Formed mainly from British prisoners of war, this force, later to be renamed the British Free Korps, saw very little active service, although a number of its men fought and died whilst defending Berlin. One of them, Thomas Haller Cooper, joined the Adolf Hitler Division of the Waffen *SS* and was wounded on the Russian front before returning to be made an NCO in the BFK. Captured by advancing allied troops, Cooper stood trial, was found guilty of treason, and sentenced to death. He was, however, reprieved later. Although research has been going on for a number of years, all attempts to track down an actual photograph of the BFK in uniform have proved unsuccessful. On the standard *SS* grey, they wore flashes, the letters BFC and the Union Jack flag. One obscure source does claim to have seen a photograph in Britain, which shows a group of men in uniform and wearing suitable cuff titles, but no reliable documentary evidence has so far been discovered.

Black, pre-1938 *SS* uniforms sported a swastika armband of red, white and black edged with half-inch black tape. Once the new field-grey uniform had been introduced, the armband was replaced by the *SS* emblem. The distinctive details of this emblem are the eagle's wings which terminate in pronounced feathered tips – the emblems of the other Services tend to have rounded or squared tips. The *SS* emblem was worn on the left sleeve; those of the other Services on the right breast.

As with Nazi headgear, it would be impossible to list all Nazi uniforms. Firstly because they have suffered from the ravages of time, and secondly because records after 1943–4 are incomplete. One collector has spent the past twenty-three years trying to list the uniforms of the NSDAP. So far he has managed to trace over three hundred variations and is still searching. Remember that a uniform was issued for just about any official position, be it railway porter, forester, female worker or postman, and you can see the enormity of the kind of task.

Undoubtedly the most lavish and varied uniforms were those of the *Luftwaffe*, which boasted sixteen different types for its officers, NCO's and other ranks. These were: field dress; service dress; flying service uniform; parade dress uniform; walking-out dress uniform; reporting uniform; guard uniform; summer uniform for officers; undress uniform for officers and leading NCOs; formal full-dress uniform for officers (evening); formal full-dress uniform for officers (day); informal full-dress uniform for officers (evening); informal full-dress uniform for NCOs and other ranks; formal full-dress uniform for NCOs and other ranks; physical training kit.

Also of interest and importance for collectors of uniforms, is the different, coloured piping which distinguishes the various branches of the Service. This is known as *Waffenfarbe* and, roughly translated, means 'Service colour'. It can be traced back to the days of the Boxer Rising in 1900, when Germany dispatched troops to China wearing, for the first time, decorations bearing colours to distinguish the different branches of the Service. Although this piping can be found on uniforms dating back to the 1830s and 1870s, these examples cannot really be classed as true *Waffenfarbe*. Here is a guide to the different colours.

Carmine　Army Veterinary Academy; Veterinary officers, NCOs and troops; Veterinary inspection and research establishments; War Academy.
Bright red　Generals; Mounted artillery units; Artillery observation units; Artillery

training regiments; Artillery regiments; Artillery School; Artillery NCOs School; Experimental command Hillesleben; Experimental command Kummersdorf; Ordnance Technician School; School for Artificers; Army Ordnance Director.

White   Machine-gun battalions; Army map and military survey personnel; Army group command; General command; Bandmasters; Recruiting office personnel; Infantry divisional staff; Infantry regiments; Infantry regiment 'Grossdeutschland'; Garrison Battalion of Vienna; Infantry School; War College; Army Sports School; NCOs schools; Mortar battalions; Army anti-aircraft units; Motorcycle units; NCOs Preparatory School; Infantry training regiments; NCOs and men of the Staff of the Military Authority of the Reichsprotektor; Army School of Music.

Black   Railway pioneer training companies and schools; Fortress pioneer units; Pioneer battalions and pioneer training units; Pioneer NCOs School; Technical officers.

Black and white   Armoured engineer companies.

Light blue   Transport and transport training units; Transport Supply School.

Cornflower blue   Medical officers, NCOs and troops; Medical training units; Military Medical Academy; Supply officer.

Grass green   Armoured infantry regiments; Motorcycle units.

Light green   Alpine and Mountain Troops' School; Mountain troop divisional staff; Mountaineering and rifle units.

Copper brown   Motorised reconnaissance; Motorcycle units.

Orange   Military field police; Engineer Officers Academy; Recruiting personnel.

Light grey   Army propaganda troops.

Grey-blue   Specialist officers.

Bordeaux red   Army Gas School; Smoke units and training units; Army Gas Defence School; Military Justice.

Rose pink   Armoured division staff; Armoured units and training regiments; Armour School; General armoured commands and armoured trains; Rifle brigade staff; Army School of Motoring; Motor maintenance troops; Anti-tank units.

Lemon yellow   Signals training regiments, school and units; Fortress signals; Army School of Dog and Carrier Pigeon Services.

Golden yellow   Army Cavalry Schools and Cavalry units; Mounted reconnaissance; Light division staff.

Members of the Luftwaffe also wore a system of *Waffenfarbe* used in conjunction with collar patches unique to the Luftwaffe.

White   Air Vice-Marshal and upwards and by members of the General Goering Regiment.

Orange   Officers on half-pay.

Gold brown   Signals.

Black   Air Ministry.

Rose   Engineer corps.

Yellow   Flight personnel.

Red   Artillery, anti-aircraft and ordnance.

Dark green   *Wehrmachtbeamten* (other than Corps of Navigational Experts and Airfield Control).

Light green   Aircraft Control.

Carmine   General staff.

   The following branches wore additional colours.

Yellow   Worn on epaulettes as second underlay by Corps of Navigational Experts.

Bright red   Worn as an edging to collar badges by NCOs and ORs of the General Goering Regiment.

Dark red   Worn as a second underlay on epaulettes by *Wehrmachtbeamten* of the Military Supreme Court.

Light blue   Worn by *Wehrmachtbeamten*, officers and engineers of the Reserve, as a second underlay on epaulettes and collar piping.

In nearly all branches of the Services, epaulettes were given additional letters or numbers to indicate the exact branch or unit the wearer belonged to. For example, a soldier, wearing a black epaulette with rose-pink *Waffenfarbe* and the letter 'L' with button numbered '7', would have belonged to the 7th Company Panzer Instruction and Demonstration unit, having the rank of *Panzerschütze* (see *German Army Uniforms and Insignia 1933–1945* by Brian L. Davis).

ARMBANDS, CUFFBANDS OF NAZI GERMANY

Armbands and cuffbands played an important part in the structure of the Third Reich, and were worn by nearly all members of the different branches of the Party. Organisations with lengthy titles were usually condensed into a few cryptic letters. Here is a list of the different organisations that one is likely to encounter whilst searching for Nazi items.

BDM   *Bund deutscher Mädchen* (German Girls' League).

DAF   *Deutsche Arbeitsfront* (German Labour Front).

DAV   *Deutscher Auslandsverein* (National Union of Germans Abroad).

DJ   *Deutsches Jungvolk* (German Youth).

DRK   *Deutsches Rotes Kreuz* (German Red Cross).

HJ   *Hitler-Jugend* (Hitler Youth).

NSADA   Nat. Soz. Altere Deutsche Abiturienten (National Socialist League of Older German Students).

NSBDT   Nat. Soz. Bund Deutscher Techniker (National Socialist League of German Technicians).

NSBO   Nat. Soz. Bauerorganization (National Socialist Farmers' Organisation).

NSDA   Nat. Soz. Deutsche Arzte (National Socialist German Doctor's League).

NSDAP   Nat. Soz. Deutsche Arbeiterpartei (National Socialist German Worker's Party).

NSDF   Nat. Soz. Deutsche Frauen (National Socialist German Women Workers).

NSFK   Nat. Soz. Fleiger korps (National Socialist Flying Corps).

NSKK   Nat. Soz. Kraftfahrn korps (National Socialist Vehicle Corps).

NSKOV   Nat. Soz. Kriegsopferverein (National Socialist Organisation for Relief of War Victims).

NSL   Nat. Soz. Lehrer (National Socialist Teacher's League).

NSRDS   Nat. Soz. Reichsbund Deutscher Schwestern (National Socialist State League of German Sisters).

NSRL   Nat. Soz. Reichsbund für Leibesübung (National Socialist State League for Physical Training).

OT   Organization Todt (Dr Todt's Labour Service).

RAD   Reichsarbeitsdienst (State Labour Service).

RDF   Reichsbund Deutscher Familien (State League of German Families).

RLB   Reichsluftschutzbund (State Air Raid Service).

SA   Sturmabteilung (Storm Troops or Brown Shirts).

SD   Sicherheitsdienst (Security Service).

SS   Schutzstaffel (Élite Guard).

TENO   Technische Nothilfe (Emergency Technical Assistance).

WHW   Winterhilfswerk (Winter Relief Work – a compulsory 'charity').

Waffen SS   Élite Guard Forces – combat.

It would be almost impossible to list all the known armbands of that period, but a few well worth collecting are:

Deutsches Jugend (German Youth)   Armband of red with white centre stripe and black lightning rune upon a white diamond.

NSDAP   General issue armband of red, with black swastika on a white circle.

Deutscher Volkssturm Wehrmacht (Home Guard)   Red and black armband with white lettering and eagle. This could be classed as a cuffband for it was worn on the left forearm above the turn-back cuff.

Im Dienst der Deutschen Wehrmacht (In the Service of German Armed Forces) White armband with black lettering.

Tag der Wehrmacht (Armed Forces' Day)   White armband with black lettering.

47

Armband for Armed Forces   White armband with black Wehrmacht eagle.

German Veterans' League   Black armband bearing black Iron Cross with black swastika in centre, upon a red shield.

Labour Corps (RAD)   Brown armband with silver trim, eagle mounted on wreath with spade, wheat ears and swastika.

Hitler-Jugend (Hitler Youth)   Red armband with white centre stripe and black swastika on white diamond.

NSADA (National Socialist Students League)   Red armband with two white outer stripes, black swastika on white diamond.

RLB (Reich Air Defence)   Blue armband with white sunburst star, the letters RLB and swastika in centre.

NSDAP Kreis Mainz SB (Party, Mainz District, Defence Roads)   Grey armband with black lettering.

Official and State employees (Post Office, etc)   Black eagle and swastika on yellow armband.

Reichsbahn-Kraftwagen-dienst (State Chauffeurs' Service)   White armband with black lettering and red winged-wheel with DR above.

Kampf-Richter (Manoeuvres' Referee)   White armband with black lettering.

Wehrmacht-Dolmetscher (Armed Forces' Interpreter)   Narrow pink armband with black lettering.

Sanitatsman (Sanitary or Corpsman)   White armband with black and red lettering, eagle and swastika with the letters DR; pharmacist, blue armband with yellow cross.

Landwacht (Land Observer)   White armband with black lettering, also bears the official Party stamp.

Ordnance Inspector   Red armband with large white 'W'.

Deutsches Rotes Kreuz (German Red Cross)   White armband with red cross and black lettering.

Bahnhofswache (Railway Guard)   Yellow armband with black lettering.

Bau-u, Stortrupp (Defence and Barricade Troops)   Green armband with black lettering; also bears official Party stamp.

Some branches of the Luftwaffe wore a dark blue cuffband with lettering in silver embroidery, on the right sleeve. Those who had seen service in World War 1 with the Richthofen Fighting Command or the 2nd Boelcke Fighting Squadron wore this cuffband with details and date in silver. The 1st Parachute Jäger-Regiment had silver lettering upon a light-green background. Officers of the General Göering Regiment had bright silver, braid lettering and edging on their cuffbands, while their NCOs had the same insignia with a matt finish. Luftwaffe cuffbands of interest to collectors include: Geschwader General Wever; Geschwader Hindenburg;

Geschwader Boelcke; Geschwader Horst Wessel.

For the would-be specialist in cuffbands of the *SS* or the SA, a vast selection is on hand, so vast, indeed, as to form a collection on their own. It is advisable to consult *Uniforms of the SS*, vols 1–6, published by the Historical Research Unit, London. This work includes many interesting stories behind the cuffbands; for instance, that *SS-Ehrenführers* (SS Honorary Leaders), were, in the main, leading industrialists, financiers or aristocrats who had this honorary rank conferred on them by Reichsführer Heinrich Himmler. The insignia of this rank was woven in silver or aluminium wire on a pale lemon backing. A rarity to look for, is the silver and red cuffband of the *Oberste SA-Fuhrung* (SA High Command), 1933, this being the period when the *SS* came under the overall command of the SA.

The commemorative names which appear on *SS* cuffbands were those of early Nazis, killed in running battles with the Communists during the troubled times of 1923–33. Generally speaking, *SS* officers wore cuffbands, stripes and insignia with the legend and rank badges picked out in aluminium, while *SS* men had theirs picked out in white silk or cotton. As the war progressed and supplies became scarce, some *SS* units had their badges and cuffbands manufactured by local factories. As a result, many strange examples have come to light, with origins as far away as Finland, Courland and even Russia.

15. Collection of seven *SS* cuff titles

A selection of *SS* cuffbands which would form the basis of a good collection are: Hans Purps; Seidel Dittmarsch; Julius Schreck; Fritz Weitzel; Bernd; Rosemeyer; Adolf Hoh; Fritz Schulz; Friedrich Schlegel; Kurt von der Ahe; Andreas Zinkl; Ludwig Frisch; Ernst Ludwig; Paul Berek; Karl Vobis; Gerhard Landmann; Karl Ostberg; Fritz Borawski; Josef Bleser; Hans Cyranka; Oskar Goll; Frederick Karpinski; Reichsführung-*SS*; *SS*-Hauptamt and RNS-Hauptamt.

With these cuffbands, one can also collect the various .*SS* collar patches and epaulettes or shoulder straps. Indeed, it would be easy to devote all one's spare time, money, energy and resources to the *SS* alone. Its multiplicity of branches, ranging from the *Waffen SS, Allgemeine SS, Germanische SS, SS-Verfugungstruppe,* to the notorious *SS-Totenkopfverbände* could absorb a lifetime of collecting.

Many of the recruits for *SS* regiments came from the ranks of the two youth organisations, the DJV and the HJ. Recruits who measured up, after first serving as an *SS Bewerber* (applicant), and fulfilling all regimental obligations, were sworn into the *SS* on the 9th November – 'Party Day'. Thereafter, they were allowed to wear the *SS* dagger engraved with the *SS* moto, *Meine Ehre Heisst Treue* (My honour is loyalty). Since it was a strictly Nazi organisation, the ranks were different to those of any other military sector.

To aid the collector to identify the many pieces of *SS* insignia, here is a table relating ranks and military organisations.

SS	*German Army*	*British Army*
Reichsführer	Generalfeldmarschall	Field-Marshal
Oberstgruppenführer (from 1942)	Generaloberst	No equivalent
Obergruppenführer	General	General
Gruppenführer	Generalleutnant	Lieutenant-General
Brigadeführer	Generalmajor	Major-General
Oberführer	Oberst	Brigadier
Standartenführer	Oberst	Colonel
Obersturmbannführer	Oberstleutnant	Lieutenant-Colonel
Sturmbannführer	Major	Major
Haupstürmführer	Hauptmann	Captain
Obersturmführer	Oberleutnant	Lieutenant
Untersturmführer	Leutnant	2nd Lieutenant
Stürmscharführer	Stabsfeldwebel	Regimental Sergeant-Major
Stabsscharführer	Hauptfeldwebel	Sergeant-Major
Oberscharführer	Feldwebel	Quartermaster-Sergeant
Scharführer	Unterfeldwebel	Staff Sergeant

Unterscharführer	Unteroffizier	Sergeant
Rottenführer	Obergefreiter	Corporal
Stürmann	Oberschütze	Lance-Corporal
SS-Mann	Schütze	Private
SS Anwärter		Candidate

Ranks for the Luftwaffe are also somewhat complex so a list with British counterparts are included.

Luftwaffe	Royal Air Force
Generalfeldmarschall	Marshal of the Air Force
Generaloberst	Air Chief Marshal
General der Flakartillerie	No equivalent
General der Flieger	No equivalent
Generalleutnant	Air Marshal
Generalmajor	Air Vice-Marshal
Oberst	Group Captain
Oberstleutnant	Wing Commander
Major	Squadron Leader
Hauptmann	Flight Lieutenant
Oberleutnant	Flying Officer
Leutnant	Pilot Officer
Stabsfeldwebel	No equivalent
Oberfahnrich	No equivalent
Oberfeldwebel	Flight Sergeant
Fahnrich	Flight Ensign
Unteroffizier	Sergeant
Hauptgefreiter	Corporal
Obergefreiter	Leading aircraftman
Fahnenjunker-Gefreiter	Flight cadet lance corporal
Gefreiter	Aircraftman, 1st class
Fleiger	Aircraftman, 2nd class

With the coming to power of the Nazi Party in 1933, a whole new field of military and para-military organisations came into being, and with them a multitude of badges and insignia. Many were adopted from those used in World War 1. Others were a mixture of designs found on shields carried by the old Nordic warriors and Hitler's concept of a new Germany.

For many of the important battles and engagements there was a sleeve badge issued made from either thin brass or tin.

51

CRIMEA   A tin shield, brassed, bearing a map with 'KRIM, 1941–2', spread eagle looking right, swastika and wreath below.

KUBAN   As for the Crimea but with large 'KUBAN' and '1943' in centre.

CHOLM   Tin shield, brassed, bearing hunched eagle looking left on an Iron Cross and swastika, and 'CHOLM 1942' beneath.

LAPLAND   Tin shield, brassed, bearing map, 'LAPLAND' and hunched eagle above looking right.

NARVIK   Long tin shield, brassed, bearing crossed anchor and aeroplane propeller, alpine flower, '1940' and 'NARVIK', the whole surmounted by a hunched eagle looking left with wreath and squared swastika beneath.

DEMJANSK   Another long tin or brass shield, bearing in the centre crossed swords, aeroplane, '1942' and DEMJANSK', the whole surmounted by a hunched eagle, swastika and wreath.

In Nazi Germany, many of the awards and badges could be classed as a form of medal being won in combat or defence positions. During the early part of the war, these Assault badges or Combat clasps were manufactured in a heavy brass or alloy. However, as the war progressed and the need for metals became a matter of some importance, these awards became somewhat thinner and lighter – so much so that, by 1945, they resembled pieces of stamped out sardine cans. Indeed there is an example known as the Lorient shield which was manufactured at the local fish cannery in 1944. For further details see *Orders, Decorations, Medals and Badges of the Third Reich* by C. M. Dodkins and David Littlejohn.

Among these assault clasps, the most interesting are:

GENERAL ASSAULT   Oval alloy badge consisting of oak wreath with hunched Wehrmacht eagle and swastika with crossed bayonet and stick-grenade beneath. Originally issued to assault engineer units in June 1940.

GENERAL ASSAULT, 25 ENGAGEMENTS   Almost identical with the previous badge, but a little larger and with '25' at the base.

PANZER ASSAULT, 50 ENGAGEMENTS   Oval wreath with hunched Wehrmacht eagle and swastika, tank bearing right with '50' in plaque beneath.

PANZER ASSAULT, 75 ENGAGEMENTS   Almost identical with the above, but with large sprays of oak leaves on either side of the '75' plaque.

ARMY ANTI-AIRCRAFT   Oval wreath with hunched Wehrmacht eagle and swastika at top, AA gun facing left.

INFANTRY ASSAULT   Oval wreath with hunched Wehrmacht eagle and swastika at top, rifle and bayonet facing left; issued in bronze, silver, gold.

AIR FORCE FLAK   Oval wreath with Luftwaffe eagle and swastika facing left and AA gun facing right.

NAVAL ARTILLERY   Oval wreath with hunched eagle and swastika facing left, heavy

16. Four NSDAP awards: *left to right* army anti-aircraft; panzer assault; general assault; sports badge

artillery piece facing left.

BLOCKADE RUNNER Round badge with silver chain design along edge, large, grey, matt-finish ship with silver eagle and swastika on bow. (I have seen a presentation set which included a miniature award).

U-BOAT COMBAT Small brass oval badge with eagle and swastika at top and U-boat in centre spread left to right.

AUXILIARY CRUISER Oval wreath with outspread eagle and swastika at the top; centre bears the globe with a Viking ship ploughing through the waves.

FLEET SERVICE Gilt oval wreath with outspread eagle and swastika at the top, large battleship steaming full ahead in centre.

MINESWEEPER Oval wreath with outspread eagle and swastika at the top, centre bearing a plume of water from exploded mine.

TORPEDO BOAT Gilt oval wreath with outspread eagle and swastika at the top; centre bearing speeding torpedo boat facing left.

AIR FORCE PARACHUTIST Oval wreath with swooping eagle plunging left, clutching swastika in its talons. Army parachutists were also eligible for this award, but this clasp had a Wehrmacht eagle at the top of the wreath.

GLIDER PILOT Oval wreath with soaring eagle rising to right; swastika mounted at the base of wreath.

RADIO OPERATOR Oval wreath with swooping eagle facing left, clutching lightning bolts in its talons; swastika mounted at base of wreath.

Apart from these clasps, it was possible to win military decorations for individual skill at arms under battle conditions, for example: the special badge for single-handed destruction of a tank; the badge for shooting down low-flying aircraft; and the Sniper's Badge (three grades).

Wound badges, issued in World War 1, are in the form of an oval wreath, with a steel helmet mounted upon a pair of crossed swords. They came in three classes: black for one to two wounds; silver for three to four wounds; and gold for five or more wounds. Badges won in 1939-45 are similar, except that the helmet bears the swastika. A rare wound badge is that awarded to members of the Condor Legion who fought for General Franco in Spain during the Civil War; only 182 were issued, all in 1936. Even rarer is the wound badge issued on 20 July 1944. After the abortive attempt on Hitler's life, three classes were awarded: gun-blue and silver; silver; and gold. According to existing records, only 11 recipients received this solid silver (·800 fine) badge which bore on the obverse the usual steel helmet, swastika, crossed swords and laurel wreath. It differs from the early patterns in having, beneath the helmet, '20 JULI 1944', and a facsimile of Adolf Hitler's signature. Fakes do exist but they are rather poorly finished and without the L/12 800, mark on the reverse. The Naval wound badge was oval with crossed swords superimposed on an anchor, the whole surrounded by an oval of anchor chain.

Among the Combat badges to search for are:

SUBMARINE CLOSE COMBAT   A slim breast badge of an oval wreath with submarine in centre, eagle and swastika above, oak-wings on either side.

LUFTWAFFE DIVEBOMBER   Round badge with oak-wings either side; centre has a winged arrow pointing downwards towards a squared swastika (if wreath is black it indicates night flights).

LUFTWAFFE COMBAT FLIGHTS   Round wreath with oak-wings either side; centre has crossed swords above squared swastika. Pennants or bars were clipped on for number of missions accomplished.

LUFTWAFFE MILITARY RECONNAISSANCE   Round wreath with oak-wings either side; centre has large eagle facing left. Pennants or bars for two, three, four and five hundred flights are known to exist but are rare.

CLOSE COMBAT BAR   Wide oak-wings with outspread eagle and swastika above a crossed bayonet and stick grenade.

NAVY FIELD COMBAT   Oval badge with oak-wings; in centre a furled anchor.

The different types of marksmanship lanyards also make a fine display.

DAGGERS AND SWORDS

The scope for building a collection of German daggers is certainly great. Almost every branch of the NSDAP, from the lads of the *Hitler-Jugend* right through to the crack *SS* troops, carried edged weapons. A quick poll of friends and family should produce the odd item, as folk die, move on or decide to sort through the mountain of family rubbish that accumulates over a period of years.

Before starting to collect, it's worth establishing what are the known scarcities and rarities. There is nothing worse then hunting and searching for one particular item with just a few pounds in your pocket, then finding it one day with a price tag way beyond your means!

High on the list for a novice will be the small *Hitler-Jugend* dagger. This is a short sheath knife (10in overall, blade 5⅜in), which was carried by members of the HJ. The single-edged blade can be found with and without the inscription *'Blut und Ehre'* (Blood and Honour), and the 'RZM M 7/9 1939' Party stamp. The scabbard is of black-painted metal, while the grip is an early form of plastic, black-chequered and inset with a red, white, gold and black diamond-shaped insignia of the HJ. The pommel and single, upswept quillion are plated. Belt fixing is from a leather loop, doubled over and fastened with two rivets to the sheath, another small strap holding the grip upright. Copies are being manufactured in Germany and shipped to Britain and USA, but close inspection will reveal a thin panel (¼in×2in), stamped with the words, 'Made in Western Germany'. Some nefarious dealers are not beyond erasing this, but a powerful magnifying glass soon overcomes that problem!

Swords and daggers of the Nazi period, as well as fine examples of the Imperial German era, are now being reproduced in that country. This has given rise to some strange situations. One manufacturer has already been taken to task for forgery, but he disputed this. Pointing to a framed licence on his office wall, he showed the authorities that the original order for manufacturing swords and dress daggers, issued before World War 1, had never been revoked. Just like the tale of sleeping beauties, a lot of rather business-like old firms have awakened after a long slumber. Even so, it is still possible to find genuine contemporary pieces which have lain undisturbed and forgotten in some dusty attic. The new examples have one 'short-coming' – the metal is much brighter and, dare I say it, has a better finish. It would appear that modern methods of smithing cannot quite capture that certain something which distinguishes those weapons of sixty and thirty years ago.

Another popular Nazi dagger is that of the infamous SA or 'Brownshirt' battalions. Measuring some 14¾in overall, weighing 18oz, with a blade of 1⅜in wide at the

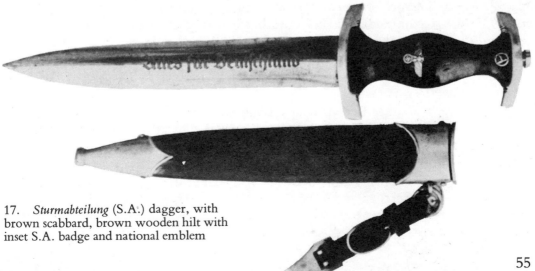

17. *Sturmabteilung* (S.A.) dagger, with brown scabbard, brown wooden hilt with inset S.A. badge and national emblem

crossguard, this dagger can be classed as one of the most popular of Nazi designs. It is thought to have been modelled on the famous sixteenth-century 'Holbein' dagger. It proved to be a very impressive-looking sidearm and also gained popularity among the hard-pressed *SS* legions on the Russian front during the bitter hand-to-hand struggles of 1941–42.

There are three main 'Holbein-style' daggers to collect. One, as already mentioned, is that of the SA, readily identifiable by its painted, stained or polished, brown, wooden hilt. This bore a small eagle and swastika and the SA button emblem, and the brown-painted sheath had German silver or nickle mounts. The blade bears the inscription '*Alles für Deutschland*', and any of a dozen makers' names. With a little luck, you may find one with the original, brown leather belt hanger. Whilst searching for one of these SA daggers, be sure to check for signs of grind marks on the blade. Ernst Röhm, leader of the SA until he fell from favour on the 'Night of the Long Knives' (30 June 1934), had a number of these daggers inscribed with his name. After his assassination, there was a frantic rush to a handy grindstone for a quick removal job! Find an original 'Ernst Röhm' blade and you have yourself a treasured piece!

Another interesting weapon is the NSKK dagger. The NSKK were the motor-cycle battalions of the SA, many of whom joined the *SS* at the outbreak of World War 2. Their dagger was almost identical with that of the SA, except for its black-painted sheath.

The third of these 'Holbein' knives is the *SS* dagger. This handy fighting weapon had a black-painted sheath, a painted or stained black wooden hilt and bore the inscription '*Meine Ehre heisst Treue*' on the blade. On the hilt it sported the eagle, swastika and small *SS* runic button. Mounts for the officer's pattern dagger bore linked swastika designs and the linked hanging chain carried *SS* runes and death's-head insignia. The *SS* Trooper's model carried just one hanging ring fixed to the locket, which accommodated a black leather frog or harness bearing RZM and *SS* markings. Of course there are patterns of the 'Holbein' dagger which were carried by other branches of the NSDAP, but it would take far too long to list them all here. However, Andrew Mollo provides an excellent review in *Daggers of the Third German Reich 1933–1945*.

The *Luftwaffe* boast only two daggers and a sword. The first pattern dagger is almost Viking in design with a blue leather and plated sheath. Its hanging chains are of aluminium. The blade is double-edged with a blue leather, wire-bound grip, while the pommel takes the form of a disc with a wheeled swastika mounted on either side. The quillions are of downswept wings. If you imagine this dagger grown to the size of a sword, then you have a good mental picture of the *Luftwaffe* officer's sword. However, the scabbard was hung, not from aluminium chains, but from a unique leather bucket, which was itself clipped to the sword-belt.

The second pattern dagger for *Luftwaffe* officers was introduced after 1937. It is very much smaller and arguably of inferior workmanship. Sheath and mounts are of plated metal, with the quillions formed from a swooping *Luftwaffe* eagle and swastika. The pommel is ball-shaped and consists of two swastikas mounted on either side and surrounded by oak leaves. Hanging straps of grey velvet, edged with silver braid, are mounted with alloy clips and buckles embossed with acorn and oak-leaf motif.

Very similar in design to this *Luftwaffe* dagger, the Wehrmacht dagger differs in that the quillions are smaller and in the form of the Army eagle, while the pommel is cone-shaped and has no swastikas. The hanging straps are of green velvet with $\frac{1}{2}$in silver braid and alloyed, oak-leaf-embossed fittings.

A truly splendid and ornate dagger is that of the Navy, or *Kriegsmarine*. The romance of the rolling seas is present in every twist and turn of the metal. This is no squalid essay in alloy; this piece gleams in gilded brass, and I have seen one example that boasted a sheath of heavy, hand-beaten copper. The fine, double-edged stiletto blade is forged from best Soligen steel and engraved with ships, anchors and so on. The pommel is in the form of a hunched eagle and swastika. The hilt is of white ivorine with a wire binding. A small brass stud is mounted on the crossguard, which

18. World War I Imperial German naval presentation dagger, made by J. Robrecht, Berlin, with fine damascened blade bearing inlaid gold inscription. The Nazi pommel was fitted after 1933

retains the dagger in its sheath. Rare examples of submarine service daggers do exist and can be identified by the U-Boat engraved on the blade or by the name of Admiral Doenitz. This indicates that this was a 'Naval Honour Dagger', presented to only a handful of U-Boat commanders.

Like all other *SS* paraphernalia, the swords of this élite corps are fetching very high prices, and can be reckoned to be one of the smartest of the Nazi regime. Complete in scabbard with full furniture and fittings, they are highly sought after at auction.

Very similar in design to a Police sword, which could also be issued with *SS* marks, the *SS* sword is distinguished by the twin lightning runes mounted on the hilt and sword knot. Those that do exist are usually in good condition because an order by the Reichsführer-*SS* restricted the wearing of the sword for the duration of the war.

One extremely unusual knife is the all-metal bayonet-trench knife used in both world wars. The sharp 6in stiletto blade fits snugly into its green-painted sheath, which matches the colour of the shaped metal grip. *Kampfmesser* or personal fighting knives can also be found from both wars. Designed very much like the bayonet-trench knife, this beechwood-hilted knife was housed in a stamped metal sheath with black enamel finish. It was held in place either in the jackboot or waist-belt with a patent, spring-steel clip.

Bayonets provide an almost endless list of different patterns and variations. We find German bayonets in almost every part of the globe. One that was manufactured as an export piece was the 'Kar. 98', originally intended for a South American market. With the advent of Word War 1, it was issued to German machine-gunners, and a saw-back blade variation saw service with pioneer battalions.

The Mauser M84/98 saw service in both world wars and, apart from minor changes, (bakelite grips replacing the early wood grips in 1937), stayed the same. Issued for service with the *Wehrmacht*, it also saw service with the *Waffen-SS, SA Wehrmann*, and, during the defence of Berlin, with some *Hitler-Jugend* combat units.

Nazi dress bayonets – sidearms that were not intended for actual combat – are greatly sought after, and range from those awarded as proficiency prizes to the deluxe pieces purchased privately. Many, with the blade suitably etched, were presented to senior NCOs on their retirement.

Nazi Police units also carried a rather distinctive bayonet. Housed in a leather and steel scabbard, the bayonet pommel is in the form of an eagle head. Grips are of stag-horn surmounted by the Nazi Police emblem. There are several patterns of this Police bayonet, some with a 17in blade and later models with a shorter $9\frac{5}{8}$in blade.

Apart from collecting the weapons themselves, the various sidearm knots are an interesting subject for study and collection. Known as *Troddel, Faustriemen,* and *Portepee*, these colourful knots were worn with bayonet, dagger and sabre. Dating back to the early 1800s, we find that nearly every regiment, battalion and company had this tassel with their own distinctive range of colours.

BELTS AND BUCKLES

Here again, the field is vast. Every organisation boasted a belt and buckle of one kind or another. Back in the Imperial days, buckles for NCOs and other ranks were rectangular in shape and bore the Imperial crown surrounded by the inscription 'Gott Mit Uns' ('God with Us'). These can be found in both brass and steel.

Buckles of the Nazi regime are to be found in polished or painted steel, in aluminium or in plain brass. Designs vary with the branch of the Services or Party organisation. SS buckles can nearly always be identified by the inscription 'Meine Ehre heisst Treue' and the RZM stamp on the back. Of course, with the Danish, Flemish and Dutch SS Volunteers, we encounter a number of variations in patterns. Officers' belt buckles are of the circular, interlocking variety and carry all the relevant details of branch of service or organisation. Apart from the standard-size belt and buckle, there was a smaller version worn on a trouser waistband. These are not so common as the regular $2\frac{1}{2}$in $\times$ $1\frac{3}{4}$in pattern and command a good price.

Leather equipment of both the Imperial Army and the Nazi regime is now a popular area for collectors. Belts, cross-straps and pouches that had seen service in World War 1 were utilised by the Nazi Party in the early 1920s but, after 1933, special, white leather equipment was issued to members of the SS LAH regiment, while Artillery, Engineers, Mountain troops and Bicycle squadrons had their own versions. Officers of the SS wore an aluminium braid belt which carried interwoven SS runes in the material.

FLAGS

Flags and banners suffer more than most items from the ravages of moth and time. When they are found in good order, they should be well sprayed with anti-moth mixture. The only prudent way of displaying them is out of direct sunlight and, if not behind glass, then encased in a form of clear, plastic wallet. With flags and banners of the Nazi era showing wear and tear, imagine what those of an earlier age look like! A number of years ago, I was lucky enough to buy, very cheaply, an embroidered banner of the German Old Comrades' Organisation. Finely executed in gold and silver wire on a yellow and cornflower-blue background, this banner of the 1920s had lain for years tucked away in a cupboard. Come the death of the householder, it had been tossed out with other rubbish to await the eagle eye of the refuse collector. This is a signal example of the important part that luck plays in collecting; now and again things seem to flutter down out of the blue. Indeed, the interest lies as much in the excitement of the chase, the research and the final capture of the item, as in ownership of it.

Nazi flags and banners may be 20–30ft long giants, which hung from tall office buildings, or small triangle pennants, originally displayed on vehicles. Those of the SS are very much sought after, in particular the trumpet banner of the SS-Ver-

19. *Left:* Brass belt buckle worn by an officer in the N.S.K.K., the National Motor Corps

20. *Centre:* Standard-top of the Nazi *Kyffhaüserbund* (Old Comrades Association for veterans of World War I)

21. *Right:* Pennant worn on S. A. staff officer's car

fügungstruppe or *SS-Totenkopfverbände*. These had a death's head worked in aluminium lamé, with regimental designation underneath on one side, while the other side sported a pair of *SS* runes in aluminium lamé. The Company Flag of the Norwegian *SS* is another choice piece. Sometimes found printed, there are, however, examples in double-sided silk. All have a black background with *SS* runes in the centre. On some the name of a town or city and the *SS* motto will be found.

From 1926, it became the practice to inaugurate all new flags and standards by touching them with the 'Blood Flag'. This flag had been with Hitler and his followers from the early days when street battles with the Communists were part of everyday life. When its bearer, Andreas Bauriedl, was killed by rifle fire during the Munich *Putsch* of 1923, the tattered flag was dipped into a pool of his blood. From that time, it became one of the most revered Party symbols and was paraded on every Party Day by Hitler himself.

Most Nazi flags and pennants carry an official stamp setting out in a form of code the branch of service, the type and particular use for which it was intended. Some were even manufactured for use as pall cloths or coffin drapes; these are soon identifiable from the overpowering stench of formaldehyde which, even after all these years, can still be smelt.

IMPERIAL GERMAN AND NAZI MEDALS

This is a subject so vast and complex that it would take a whole volume to cover all the awards ever issued. (See *War Medals* by Derek E. Johnson). Here we open up a field of collecting which covers nearly 135 years of Germanic history. Not only do we become involved with the many Prussian States – now swallowed up and forgotten – but we are also concerned with a period when Germany ruled the whole of Europe. There were medals and orders for nearly every branch of the mighty Nazi organisation. As we have already seen from the plethora of Nazi Assault and Combat clasps or pieces of insignia, nobody was allowed to forget that they belonged to the Party.

Many of the awards were given to volunteer divisions formed in occupied countries such as Holland, Norway, Finland, Czechoslovakia and Croatia. At the end of the war, many members of these divisions were either incarcerated in Russian labour camps, or, managing to escape the slaughter on the Eastern front, were absorbed by the Displaced Persons' Camps scattered around Europe. As they fled west, their medals and insignia were discarded or bartered for a few cigarettes and lumps of bread.

Just as the recipients of many medals in the last war were not German at all, so, curiously, one of the first medals to be struck for German soldiers, the Hanover medal, was issued by command of the Prince Regent of Great Britain. It was awarded to the surviving soldiers and to relatives of the slain from Waterloo. The medal is $1\frac{5}{8}$in in diameter and bears on the obverse the laureated head of the Prince Regent facing right, with draped truncation and surrounded by the inscription 'Georg. Prinz. Regent 1815'. On the reverse in the centre is 'Waterloo Jun XVIII', flanked by laurel wreaths, with a trophy of arms above, and encircled by the inscription 'Hanoverischer Tapferkeit'. The medal was suspended from a large steel ring and clip by means of a crimson and blue-edged ribbon, similar to the British Waterloo medal ribbon.

Another interesting medal of this period was the Brunswick Medal. This was also ordered by the Prince Regent (as guardian of the minor Princes of Brunswick), and issued to the soldiers of Brunswick who were present at the action on 16, 17, and 18 June 1815. The medal was struck in 1818 from captured French cannon. On the obverse, it bears the head of Duke Frederick Wilhelm of Brunswick, who was killed at the battle of Quatre Bras. The inscription, in Gothic script, reads 'Friedrich Wilhelm Herzog. On the reverse is the date 1815, encircled by a wreath of oak and laurel, with an inscription in German arranged round and divided by rosettes – Braunschweig Seinen Kriegern. Quatrebas und Waterloo' 'Brunswick to her Warriors. Quatre Bras and Waterloo'). The medal is $1\frac{3}{8}$in in diameter and was suspended from a steel ring and clip by a $1\frac{1}{2}$in yellow ribbon, with broad stripes near the edge. The officers' medals were gilt, with their names engraved on the edge.

A war between the Prussians and the Austrians, which lasted just seven weeks and ended in complete victory for the Prussians, showed the world how far superior the breech-loading, needle-fire rifle was against the outdated muzzle-loader used by the

Austrians. At the battle of Sadowa, the Austrians lost 20,000 men killed or wounded, with just as many taken prisoner. The Prussian losses were 10,000.

The medal struck to commemorate this conflict was called the Prussian König Gratz Cross 1866. The Cross bears in the centre the Royal Cypher w.R., surrounded by the legend *'Preussen Siegreichem Heere'* ('To Prussia's victorious army'). On the upper arm of the Cross, is the Prussian crown, on the left arm *'War uns Sei'*, on the right arm *'Gott mit Ihm'*, and on the lower section *'Die Ehre'*. On the reverse, is the crowned Prussian eagle, sitting on a cannon. On the upper arm, is *'König-Gratz'*, on the right *'Juli'*, on the left *'Denz'*, and on the lower, *'1866'*. The ribbon is of black corded silk, 1in wide, with narrow stripes of white and orange at the edges.

The 1813 Prussian Iron Cross – the Cross which was to lay the foundation for all future Iron Crosses – was instituted by King Frederick William III on 10 March 1813 to reward those, either military or civilian, who had distinguished themselves in the war of that time. It was divided into three classes for both soldiers and civilians. The Grand Cross, which was double the size of the Knight's Cross and worn round the neck, was awarded exclusively for the winning of a decisive battle, the capture of an important position or the brave defence of a fortified position. The recipients of the Cross 1st Class would also wear upon the left breast a similar Cross or Badge. Regulations governing the award of this Cross allowed all ranks to be eligible.

The decoration is a cast-iron cross pattée, with silver borders and mountings. On the obverse, in the centre within a silver, milled border, are three oak leaves; above, 'FR' surmounted by the Prussian crown, below, '1813'. For the Cross worn by the military, the ribbon was black with two white stripes near the edge; and for that worn by civilians, white with black edges.

At the close of hostilities, the Cross was suspended but was reintroduced on 19 July 1870 for the Franco-Prussian War. The Cross awarded for the 1870 war differs in that it has in the centre of the reverse, also within a silver, milled border, the initial 'W', with a crown above, and below, '1870'. Recipients of this award who were awarded another during the 1914–18 war received a bar with a miniature cross superimposed. This, however, was only worn on the ribbon of a Cross 2nd Class.

The origins of the Iron Cross make for interesting reading. It appears that back in the Napoleonic Wars, the women of Germany, anxious to help with the war effort, hit upon the idea of giving up their jewellery to help pay for arms and equipment. Once bereft of conventional jewellery, they hung themselves about with iron ornaments. These delicate pieces were, incidentally, genuine works of art and, today, can be viewed alongside the many other treasures in the Victoria and Albert Museum, London. Appropriately, as a mark of respect to the women of Germany, the medal ordered by the King was executed in iron.

One of the many rules governing the medal decreed that the Iron Cross 2nd Class should be worn from the buttonhole with the crowned 'FW', oak leaves and '1813' showing. The award was, however, usually worn with the reverse side showing, and, in 1938, the common practice was recognised and officially sanctioned. Another important condition was that a 1st Class award could only be made if the 2nd Class had already been won. The elaborate etiquette which defined eligibility and correct mode of display did not, it seems, weary the authorities into a niggardly attitude to the award; over five million Iron Crosses 2nd Class, and about 218,000 1st Class medals were awarded in World War 1.

The next significant change was made in 1939, when Hitler upgraded the Iron Cross to the status of an Order. This Cross bears on the obverse a swastika in the centre, and '1939' on the lower arm. The reverse has a plain black area, with '1813' on the lower arm. The ribbon was also modified; the centre has a wide, red stripe with a black–and–white stripe on either side. The 1st Class medal has a plain silver back, with either a vertical brooch-pin or a screw-back fitting for wearing on the left breast-pocket. At the time of World War 2 then, the Order was organised into: Grand Cross (64mm×64mm); Knight's Cross, with golden oak leaves and swords, and brilliants (48mm×48mm); Knight's Cross, with silver oak leaves and swords, and brilliants; Knight's Cross, with oak leaves and swords; Knight's Cross with oak leaves; Knight's Cross; Iron Cross 1st Class (44mm×44mm); Iron Cross 2nd Class (44mm×44mm).

The Grand Cross and the Knight's Crosses were worn at the throat, while the Iron Cross 1st Class was pinned on the left breast without a ribbon, and the Iron Cross 2nd Class was worn, together with other awards, on a bar above the left breast. Recipients of the 1914 Iron Cross who also won a 1939 type were allowed to wear their original award, but with an eagle and swastika bar mounted on the ribbon of the 2nd Class award or clipped to the tunic above the 1st Class medal.

Among the many thousands who won the Iron Cross was Adolf Hitler, who was awarded the 1st Class Cross in 1917. One of the youngest holders of the Knight's Cross was Günther Nowack, just sixteen years old, a member of the *Hitler-Jugend* seconded into the ranks of the Volkssturm towards the end of World War 2. Alone, he disabled nine Russian tanks by placing linked grenades in vulnerable positions as they lumbered by his fox-hole. After the final surrender, he was taken prisoner and shipped to a Russian POW camp where he was to die. An English double agent, Eddie Chapman, who spied for the highest bidder, was also among those entitled to wear the Iron Cross.

Apart from these especially noteworthy recipients, there were six million or more winners of 2nd Class crosses, and about 750,000 winners of the 1st Class medal in World War 2. This means that the Iron Cross is by no means rare, but it does not mean that every 'example' is necessarily genuine. If you are purchasing one of these or any other relic of the Imperial or NSDAP regime, be vigilant and, if possible, arm yourself with a knowledgeable friend.

3 Military miniatures and Bronzes

Television is to blame! Count the number of programmes in which the hero, or villain, works out tactical moves on a wargamer's table. Whether he is a retired army officer, or a smooth, well-to-do crook skulking in a luxury penthouse, he always seems to have a goodly supply of expensive, handmade, military miniatures stacked on plate glass shelves.

Military miniatures or, if you want to raise a howl of wrath from the enthusiast, toy soldiers, can be traced back to ancient times; the baking sands of Egypt produce ancient examples fashioned in wood, clay and stone. One of the finest and most interesting sets, fashioned in wood and finished with a coating of red clay, was discovered in a tomb near Meir. Although they can hardly be classed as miniatures – they are about 5ft tall – this impressive group form a formidable model bodyguard, armed, as they are, with an array of contemporary weapons.

During the Middle Ages, military miniatures very similar in design to chess pieces were used by kings or army chiefs for working out tactical manoeuvres. Later, they were used as display models for new uniforms and equipment. Materials vary and examples exist in gold, silver, pottery, wood, papier-mâché and, from Germany, an early form of plastic wood (being a mixture of sawdust and fish-glue). Although the chances of actually acquiring such early models are remote, there are numerous eighteenth- and nineteenth-century examples available at a price. However, if you cannot afford to own them, you can at least look at fourteenth- and sixteenth-century figures in a number of museums. One particularly fascinating model of a knight, a flat moulded in lead, is in the Cluny Museum in France, and a tilting knight, mounted on a wooden horse, is in the Bavarian National Museum, Munich.

Although good examples come from other countries, Germany can claim the honour of being the home of good-quality, early, model soldiers. German manu-facturers had a flair for fine detail and, during the seventeenth century, took the lead over their French counterparts, designing and manufacturing soldiers which not only boasted articulated limbs but also automatic mechanisms which enabled them to carry out simple manoeuvres. Of course, the rich and privileged classes gave their children model soldiers of silver, tin, and lead, while those of the downtrodden

22. Scale model of a 19th century ship's cannon. The barrel is cast in iron

masses were lucky to have a crudely carved, wooden 'peg-top' warrior. Not until about 1775 do we find a general influx of marketed tin soldiers. The credit for this increase must go to the Hilpert family, who established themselves in Nuremburg at that time. Soon, other German firms began to spring up and, by the mid-nineteenth century, a number of modellers had established successful businesses. This concentration of manufacturers explains the famous 'Nuremburg size' of 30mm, which became widely accepted and is still used today. Apart from this surviving standard, there were 5–6cm pieces, another size common in models.

Back in those days, children fought pitched battles with their miniature armies, emulating their elders to the alarming extent of blasting their Lilliputian troops to pieces with tiny, but deadly cannon. Unlike today's toy field pieces, which operate by means of a compressed spring, antique pieces were discharged with a minute pinch of black gunpowder. Ramming home the wad and little cannon-ball, our junior general would apply a hot match or poker to the touch-hole and wait for the whistling missile to cut down his enemy's legions. It proved a hazardous pastime. In the general excitement and confusion of battle, these projectiles sometimes missed the intended toy target, hitting a kindergarten companion instead.

Whenever a battle was won it was common practice for towns and villages to celebrate the win with a mammoth firework display and the discharging of model cannon. Time and time again, we read in contemporary newspapers of terrible accidents in which men or boys, having mishandled the loading or priming of a piece, have blown themselves to bits. One such report in the *Ipswich Journal* of 27 October 1804 reads

'On Sat. afternoon the son of a respectable man, living near Dean's-yard, West-minster, was literally blown up by gunpowder. The boy had purchased a small brass cannon, which he had in his outer-coat pocket, on his right side. He also procured a quantity of saltpetre, which he dissolved in water, and sat down by the kitchen fire, with pieces of paper, in order to make matches for firing his cannon.

'He dipped the paper into the liquid, and dried the pieces before the fire; he then twisted them and put them into his pocket, where the powder was; but, before so doing, he lighted them at one end, to ascertain whether the liquid in which he had dipped the matches was strong enough. Unluckily he omitted to extinguish one of the matches, which communicated to the others, and the powder exploded in his pocket. It blew off the whole side of his coat and waistcoat, burning his breeches, and dreadfully scorched his right side, the side of his head, and knocked him on the stove. Both eyes are much injured; but there is a prospect of his surviving.'

The expensive German figures with which the sons of the rich amused themselves were in stark contrast with the wood or tin soldiers which the rank-and-file children used until the introduction of the cheaper lead flats. The first of these were crude, two-dimensional models, cast from an alloy of tin and lead. Initially formed with just the barest detail, they soon evolved into tiny works of art (20mm), showing intricate detail and portraying even buttons, belt, swords and, by the time of the Third China War (1900), regimental facings or *Waffenfarbe*.

Both early and more recent lead flats are now much sought after by wargamer and collector alike, and, consequently, the price for a complete set has risen astronomically. As in all other areas of collecting, the forger and counterfeiter have moved in on the market. Using original figures as master-moulds, they cast almost perfect copies. However, although wax and plaster castings duplicate most of the details, they do tend to lose out on the fine lettering which is usually to be found on the base-plate. This lettering, which on the original figure is bold and proud, was intended as a form of manufacturer's code mark. Examples are: s.m.k.a.90lb (running grenadier); s.d.10a.k. (running infantryman); s.d.50b. (machine-gun supplier); s.m.k.z.90ic (shot or wounded grenadier); s.d.50a.k. (machine-gun team); e.5.k (mounted cavalry); s.d.85a.k. (gunner with lanyard); k.z.902b (running grenadier, arm raised); s.d.102 (ammunition carrier); s.d.100k. (officer at attention); k.z.907b. (kneeling, pointing bugler); s.d.100b.k. (running, shot or wounded soldier). Paint is yet another important deciding factor in the identification of these old lead soldiers. At the time of manufacture, it was common practice to use a paint carrying a high lead content, whereas today's enamels are manufactured with a lead-free, plastic base.

A very popular set of soldiers are those executed in a form of plastic wood.

23. Rare group of German models
of the Nazi period (1933–45): S.A.
flag bearer; Adolf Hitler;
N.S.D.A.P. standard bearer

Moulded on a wire frame with very realistic accoutrements they cover a wide range of German military history. A few have survived the carnage of two wars, and a comrade who was stationed in Berlin during the 1960s was lucky enough to get a few. Striking up a friendship with a German Naafi girl whose home was in the Communist-held Eastern Sector, she managed to smuggle out an incomplete set of these soldiers. They ranged from Frederick the Great, mounted on horseback complete with his famous crutch and guarded by a squad of his famous Prussian Blues, to General von Mackensen, and Herman Göring in full Luftwaffe dress uniform. The prize piece, Adolf Hitler, she wouldn't bring through the checkpoint for she reckoned if she had been searched by the East German guards she would have been shipped off to Siberia for life! If you are lucky enough to find any of these models, take care to keep them out of extreme temperatures – they tend to suffer from the elements which cause shrinkage cracks and distortion.

And so it was that the Continent led the field in manufacturing toy and model soldiers. Great Britain may have been the leading industrial country at the time, but it was not until 1893 that we find a British maker issuing any kind of serious challenge. With a name like William Britain he could hardly go wrong! Setting up shop in a window of the famous London toyshop, Gamages, he introduced his first

24. Two model soldiers made by William Britain

set – a mounted troop of hollow-cast Life Guards. Packed in a glossy red box with a smart descriptive label, they were to become the pride and joy of nearly every young lad. In 1907, A Royal Field Artillery gun, limber, horses and gunner could be bought for the price of two Sunday papers.

Over the years we find a great number of different types joining the growing ranks: 1st Bombay Lancers; 3rd Madras Light Cavalry; 1st Life Guards; 2nd Dragoons; and the 21st Empress of India's Lancers, all portrayed in colourful splendour. Britain not only specialised in exact and precise historical detail, he also had an eye on the battles and minor wars that raged around the globe at the turn of the century. Depicting the fighters and furniture of the Boer War, we find a horse-drawn ambulance complete with driver, stretcher-bearers and wounded, together with a set of long-gowned, round-based, nurses. A set of these in its original box and in first-class condition can realise about £50 ($100) by today's prices. Later, during World War 1, the same horse-drawn ambulance was again issued only this time with up-to-date khaki-clad attendants and drivers. And so the review rolls on. From the Russo-Japanese conflict, he produced two boxes of Russians and two boxes of Japanese. The latter are unique, having small gummed, circular labels stuck on the base-plate, carrying the trade name and date, 1904.

William Britain did not content himself with moulding his figures in the usual traditional poses of running, lying, standing or fighting. He introduced a whole new concept with walking wounded, dead, and stretcher cases, adding such realistic touches as a blood-stained bandage round a head or limb; the wounded warrior lying on his side or back with his topee shading his eyes from the scorching sun.

Up to World War I, toy soldiers reflected all the pomp and pageantry of Great Britain's past glory: colourful marching bands; proud, prancing Lancers, Hussars or

25.   A selection of Britain's mounted model soldiers – just part of a 500-strong collection!

26.   Hand-finished 54mm model of German cavalry officer of the Nazi period

Dragoons – each miniature troop almost looking as though they could come alive at the toot of a magic trumpet, so realistically were they modelled! With the advent of the Great War and its wholesale slaughter, not even William Britain could make the drab khaki uniforms or strange-looking motorised transport anywhere near as glamorous or appealing as those of their predecessors. Here in all its ugliness was the true face of twentieth-century warfare; one look at a set of World War 1 machine-gunners mounted on motorcycle and sidecar will illustrate the point.

Of course, Britain's models were extensively copied but one has only to compare the workmanship of the original article with the copy to appreciate the art. One must also remember that Britain did also bring out cheaper versions of his models, which, besides being slightly reduced in size, were not as meticulous in their painted detail.

For the collector, display of his 'military miniatures', as toy soldiers are now soberly titled, is as important as collection. Single or set pieces (usually consisting of just two to three items) can be displayed in a small, glass-fronted show-case. A popular size for these cases is the 54mm figure, the true collector's piece, regimentally correct right down to the last button or medal ribbon. The magazine *Tradition* will give you some idea of this impressive accuracy. Its pages reveal bold, lifelike vignettes of actual engagements, whether they took place at Waterloo or Trafalgar.

Displaying your models is a matter of individual taste, but, nevertheless, dust, dirt and exposure to strong sunlight can destroy long hours of exacting work spent in

27.   Model of a Rolls-Royce armoured car, executed in silver and presented to Commander
O. Locker Lampson by the men of the Royal Naval Air Service Armoured Car Division at a
reunion dinner in 1919

collecting or creating the models. It is certainly advisable to mount them under
either a clear-glass or plastic dome or, failing this, a small, glass-fronted box.

Aspiring artists among you may wish to try your hand at building and constructing
your own figures and set pieces. Such enthusiasts will find a list of manufacturers
at the end of the chapter. Adventurous craftsmen may purchase torso, head, limbs
and assortment of weapons piecemeal, so giving their model that individual pose.
All sorts of domestic odds and ends can be used in modelling these figures, from an
unrolled toothpaste tube to a lolly stick or fuse wire and pipe cleaners. The one
all-purpose and indispensable commodity is barbola paste which is obtainable at most
art shops. Ideal for moulding such things as buttons, badges, or belts and harness,
this pliable material will soon harden ready for a first, base coat of paint.

Although wargames have always been prevalent among military men, it was the
two books written by that far-sighted author H. G. Wells that set the miniature
cannon ball and tiny hooves in motion on civilian tables. Entitled *Floor Games* (1911)
and *Little Wars* (1913), they set out details of miniature warfare and battle tactics
together with the general rules and regulations of fighting with military miniatures.
Played very much along the same lines as chess, the game involves the use of dice,
tape-measure and sets of rules which are drawn up before the start of hostilities.

No two games are the same; in the Battle of Waterloo for instance, the skilful use
of bayonet and grapeshot could bring about an unforeseen victory for the French,
while at the Crimea the use of rifled ·577 Enfield muskets and deadly Minie bullets
could, and did, swing the victory for the Allies. However, superior as the British

arms may have been over the Russian smooth-bore, short-ranged muskets, they would be of little use, if our table-top Cardigan should forget to bring up his supply wagons of percussion caps and Minie bullets. Indeed, in that example, lies the secret of wargaming; unless the player reads and digests well the history of a battle, then, no matter how many men or cavalry he may sport, a simple omission like a wagon of food or gunpowder may lose him the battle.

The 54mm model may suit the specialist collector but those who participate in wargames tend to prefer 20mm models. These can be mounted in sets of half a dozen on a thick cardboard base, which is more adaptable for table-top manoeuvres. These lead flats can be purchased either finished or in plain white for painting in colours of the player's own choice. Those who have a steady hand and a little knowledge may even cast their own legions. If, for example, you require fifty or so cuirassiers and possess a model worth copying, then follow these simple instructions and levy yourself a troop.

CASTING A COPY OF A FLAT

1   Take a slab of modelling clay and press in the figure to be copied, lying it on its side.

2   Build a plasticine wall about 1in high around the block of clay.

3   Grease the exposed side of the figure with cycle or machine oil.

4   Make a creamy mixture of dental plaster, fill the mould and leave it in a warm dry room for two to three days.

5   Once dry, peel off the clay. This will leave the figure embedded in the plaster.

6   Clean off any rough edges on the exposed surface of the plaster and grease the surface with a coating of vaseline. Treat exposed surface of figure with cycle oil.

7   Build up the sides of block with plasticine, making walls 1in high. Fill with dental plaster and leave in dry room for another two to three days.

8   Once dry, split the mould with the aid of a thin-bladed knife.

9   Take a bar of plumber's metal (scrap lead such as piping or broken soldiers will suffice!), and melt it down over a gas or butane burner, using an old soup ladle as a receptacle.

10   When the metal is completely molten, use a small spoon to pour a measure into the mould. Some enthusiasts hold the plaster mould in their unprotected hand; this is both dangerous and impractical, for it is quite easy to let the mould slip and shatter. A better solution is to place the mould between two pieces of cloth or leather and gently clamp in a wood vice.

11   Pour in the molten metal, taking care to do so in one fluid movement. Hesitation can cause air bubbles and creasing in the finished figure. A word of warning – ensure that all surfaces of mould and tool are free from moisture. A drop of water can cause hot lead to spurt to the ceiling!

12 When the mould is cool enough for handling, remove the figure and clean off the surplus flashing. The first few attempts will not have full details of belts, buttons or uniform creases until the mould has dried right the way through.

13 Painting is up to the individual, but on the massed ranks of the 20mm models, light touches on face and hands with a flesh-coloured paint suffice. Painting in eye, mouth and shadow details is best left to the expert or until the time that you have perfected the art, for one slip can spoil the whole effect.

Those without the means or talent to cast their own 54mm models can, nevertheless, purchase them in various stages of finish from any of the firms listed. A choice of plastic or lead is readily available, with figures ranging from Ancient Greek, Roman and Egyptian soldiers, to proud, full-armoured knights, Imperial German *Uhlan* or even a complete team of Royal Horse Artillery. Most of these models are available in kit form with interchangeable limbs and a browse through the catalogues will determine the extent of the collector's individual needs and the availability of kits to meet them.

Diehards who fight shy of modern castings can convert some of the old pre-war models into fine new creations. After much experimentation, fellow militaria collector, Ron Wigley, has perfected a method of grafting which defies detection. With the aid of a soldering iron, hacksaw, pieces of wire and a lot of practice and patience, any amateur surgeon will, likewise, soon acquire the necessary skill.

Searching for the old pre-war models in anywhere near perfect condition is something of a task but, of course, the kind of task that true collectors welcome. Many are to be found skulking in the junk box of the local bric-à-brac shop and jumble sales seem to bring the odd piece to light. Refuse collectors enjoy an advantage here, and some of them use it. A couple of years ago, one walked into my shop with a complete ambulance team from the Boer War. The only casualty was the officer who had lost his head on the undignified journey by dustcart. Other sets must still be enjoying their repose in lofts or attics, awaiting the disturbing touch of a collector's hand on their epauletted shoulders.

Of the firms who manufacture military miniatures those tried and true are listed here.

Norman Newton Ltd, Tradition, 188 Piccadilly, London W1
Rose Miniatures, 45 Sundorne Road, Charlton, London SE7
Hinton Hunt Figures, Marcus Hinton, Rowsley, River Road, Taplow, Maidenhead, Berks
Miniature Figurines, 5 Northam Road, Southampton, SO2 0NZ
Historex Agents, 3 Castle Street, Dover, Kent
Airfix Products Ltd, Haldane Place, Garratt Lane, London SW18

28. A *Rampant Colt* bronze by Alvin A.
White – the trade mark of Samuel Colt

Les Higgins Miniatures, 78 Northampton Road, Wellingborough, Northants.
When writing, please remember to include a stamped, addressed envelope.

Societies connected with collecting miniatures are to be found in most countries and lists of them can be obtained from any of the main dealers. In Britain, information on military miniatures can be obtained from: J. Ruddle Esq (Secretary), British Model Soldier Society, 22 Priory Gardens, Hampton, Middx (send SAE).

A list of collecting and wargaming magazines follows.

Dispatch (Argyle, Scotland)
Sling Shot (Southampton)
Airfix Magazine (London)
Military Modelling (London)
Battle (London)
War Games News Letter (Southampton)
Sword and Lance (Darlington)
Miniature Parade (California, USA)
Strategy and Tactics (Journal of American War Gaming)
Miniature Warfare (London)
Tradition (London)

BRONZE AND CHINA FIGURES

The transition from collecting military miniatures to much larger bronze and china pieces is more than a change in size. Not only are good examples of these big pieces

29. *Above:* Modern Dresden figure of
Le Prince Eugene

30. *Right:* Small brass figure of a Turkish warrior.
Originally this was a piece of clock furniture

much harder to find but prices are also much higher. Where these items do resemble
smaller models, however, is in the wide range which may be collected, from those
with an eighteenth-century flavour to fine works executed in silver or bronze by
Alvin A. White. Some of these figures are of as great antiquity as other model
soldiers, the oldest examples coming from Egypt, Greece, and the Roman Empire.
To acquire these, you will have to be very lucky or very rich; most of them find their
way to private art collections or museums like the Colchester Castle Museum with
its bronzes of Roman gods clad in helmets and very little else. These are, of course,
relics of the Roman occupation when Colchester – or, as it was then known,
Camulodunum – was a garrison town.

Figures within the reach of an average collector do appear on the market from
time to time, and it would be advisable to subscribe to one or two of the better-
known auction firms which specialise in these. Sotheby, Christie, Wallis & Wallis,
Weller & Dufty and Kent Arms Sales usually have a fair quota throughout the year.
Some figures are always in demand and command a high price no matter what

material they are cast in. Eternally popular are Napoleon and Prinz Eugene and another perennial favourite is Nelson. Napoleon III mounted on 'Philippe', for instance, by the French artist, Emmanuel Fremiet, would make any collection distinguished. The list of desirable pieces is a long one for most nineteenth-century artists were keen to immortalise the numerous fire-and-brimstone generals who helped build the Empires of the western world. Even Kipling's humbler but no less famous 'Tommy Atkins' is remembered in the form of a small, salt-glaze figure complete with the poet's famous ditty inscribed on the base.

Collecting any of a famous series of bronzes poses a problem of distinguishing between the various versions of the same model. For example, a bronze by, say, Auguste-Nicholas Cain, the nineteenth-century French sculptor, of Duke Karl von Braunschweig may have been reduced and reproduced in bronze, silver, or spelter (form of zinc). It is possible to find spelter figures with a metallic oxide coating which gives them the appearance of bronze. Usually fitted to a marble base, it is sometimes difficult to tell at first whether the figure is bronze or not. However, close inspection and a tap with a pencil (spelter has a dull, lead-like ring) should provide a suitable clue as to its composition.

Search long and hard and you will eventually build yourself a creditable collection. Even the furniture of brass or ormolu clocks is now sought after; for, before the present interest in antique clocks (those black-marble creations!), it was common practice to break them up and use the ornate furniture and mounts as embellishments on rather tired or plain pieces of furniture. A bizarre assortment of subjects were chosen for this undignified purpose, from blood-thirsty Zulus to charging Cossacks or dying Zouaves. Cleaned and mounted on either a marble or wooden base, they can form the basis of a unique and unusual collection.

From America came a whole range of figures. A classic example is *The Wounded Bunkie*. ('Two horses in full gallop, side by side. Each horse carries a cavalryman, one of whom has been wounded and is supported in his saddle and kept from falling by the arm of the other trooper.') This, among numerous other equestrian subjects, was the work of Frederic Remington. Also from America we have the works of Harry Jackson, Charles Russell, Robert Farrington Elwell, and, as already mentioned, Alvin A. White, who has introduced a limited edition of the Rampant Colt, the trade mark of the Colt Firearms Company.

AUCTION SALE ROOMS IN U.K. DEALING IN MILITARY BRONZES
Wallis & Wallis, 210 High Street, Lewes, Sussex
Sotheby & Co, 34 & 35 New Bond Street, London, W1A 2AA
Christie & Co, 8 King Street, London SW1Y 6QT
Weller & Dufty Ltd, 141 Bromsgrove Street, Birmingham 5
Kent Arms Sales, *Black Prince*, Bourne Road, Bexley, Kent

4 Badges, Buttons and other Insignia

Regimental cap badges, those small brass or plastic (1941–45) insignia, are now much in demand by collectors the world over. It is quite fascinating to try and work out why these comparatively ordinary pieces of militaria, costing a few pence at the time of their use, have reached the astronomical prices that are paid for some choice examples today. During the two world wars, it was the practice for small lads to cadge badges from passing troop convoys and for those who were lucky enough to have the soldiers billeted with them, the field was even wider and more varied. The insignia of the Machine Gun Corps, Liverpool Pals (Kitchener's Army), Royal Marine Light Infantry, Royal Marine Artillery and Rough Riders all took their proud place on a leather belt or in a tucker-box. Even today I meet septagenarians who produce a belt or boxful of pre-war relics. Once their pride and joy, they now part with them for a few pounds to help out a pension.

Until recently, it was possible to build a collection with fairly modest means, but as the collector of militaria turned to new themes this neglected area came under his acquisitive gaze. The results of an auction held at Colchester show just how good an investment militaria can be. A collection of some 3000 cap and helmet badges originally destined for the dustcart had been rescued and put up for sale. At this extraordinary sale, cards carrying thirty badges were being knocked down at over two hundred pounds, and individual helmet plates sold for twenty pounds or more.

It is important for anyone starting a collection of British cap badges to learn to distinguish between the different types of crowns usually found at the top of each badge. The subtle differences between a King's Crown and a Queen's Crown all have to be mastered before plunging into the vast complexities of the cap-badge world. Although the soldiers of George III, George IV and William IV all bore King's Crowns on their swords, belts, buckles and shoulder-belt plates, it was not until Queen Victoria's reign that the cap badge proper was introduced. This may be yet another innovation, like the 'Albert shako', for which we must thank Prince Albert. It is to distinguish between the various later designs of badge that catalogues and collectors journals are often full of such bizarre references as; 'QVC', 'K/C' and 'Q/C'. These refer to: Queen Victoria's Crown (from about 1898 – when cap

76

31. Selection of cap badges. *Top row* (*left to right*): Military Police (George V); Royal Military Police (Elizabeth II); York and Lancaster Regt.; *bottom row*: Royal Flying Corps; Duke of Lancaster's Own. Note the differing styles of Crown

32. 92nd Royal Highland Regt. sterling silver Shoulder Belt Plate (SBP). Note the high-ears of the Victorian pattern crown

badges became fairly standard in design – to 1901); King's Crown (Edward VII 1902–10, George V 1911–35, Edward VIII Jan.–Dec. 1936 – Abdicated – George VI 1937–52); Queen's Crown Elizabeth II 1953–.

As can be seen in the illustration, a 'QVC' has rather long ears while those of the 'K/C' tend to be rather more domed like those of a Tudor Crown. The 'Q/C' has a St Edward's Crown, having a 'dropped centre'. There are other types and variations; naval crowns, mural crowns, and the odd coronet or two, but most have a sovereign's crown. Even then, the sovereign's crown is occasionally varied; the 'QVC' is known in at least three different types and the 'K/C' shows small subtle changes especially on those that were struck abroad. It is these anomalous colonial examples that most alarm the collector. Although it is wise to be on guard when purchasing any rare or early badge, there is no need to become 'fake-happy'. It is often the case that badges which were struck while a regiment was based overseas have been badly cast in lead. I have seen badges of the Scottish Horse, Ordnance Corps and Toronto Scottish so bad that if I hadn't been certain of their provenance – they were struck in India during World War 1 – I would have dismissed them as fakes.

These deceptive but genuine articles do not, however, guarantee the rest. Fakes and restrikes are to be found, coming from as far away as Pakistan or as close to home as the Midlands. Such imitations tend to be lighter in weight than real badges and have a waxy texture. The brass slide or prong-fastener (used to clip the badge into the cap) also seems to be slimmer and of a brass that is different coloured from that of an original. But, again, beware of overzealous denunciations. Many of these suspiciously bright, new badges are the genuine relics of recently disbanded or amalgamated regiments. The stores of these regiments are sold up, so that whole boxes of new, unissued badges, buttons, shoulder titles and collar-dogs come on to the market. It is when one encounters rarer items in fine condition that one should be on guard. A sudden influx of, say, World War 1 Wandsworth Scottish (only 210 issued), or pre-1881 Glengarry badges probably indicates that someone has been extra busy in the 'lost-wax casting' business. This is a method of taking a casting from an original badge using wax.

For the novice collector, there is a completely new language to be learnt. Besides terms like 'QVC', 'K/C' and 'Q/C', one will often find in catalogues, price lists and society journals an incomprehensible abbreviations table of hieroglyphs. Here is a list of terms one is likely to encounter when corresponding with fellow collectors or dealers.

AA	Anodised aluminium
ASC	Army Service Corps
ACC	Army Catering Corps
ATS	Army Territorial Service (Women)
APC	Army Pay Corps (from 1920 'Royal' was added)
AOC	Army Ordnance Corps (from 1918 'Royal' was added)
ASR	Army Scripture Readers
AVC	Army Veterinary Corps (from 1918 'Royal' was added)
AAC	Army Air Corps
DLI	Durham Light Infantry
ER.VII	Edward Rex, Seventh
EIC	East India Company
ER.VIII	Edward Rex, Eighth
ER.II	Elizabeth Regina, Second
Fus.	Fusilier
GR.	George Rex
HAC	Honourable Artillery Company
HM.	Hall Mark (to be found on silver badges)
HP	Helmet plate
HPC	Helmet plate centre
IY	Imperial Yeomanry
KDG	King's Dragoon Guards
K/C	King's Crown

KOH	King's Own Hussars
KSLI	King's Shropshire Light Infantry
KOYLI	King's Own Yorkshire Light Infantry
NCO	non-commissioned officer
NMR	Natal Mounted Rifles
OR	other rank
Q/C	Queen's Crown
QOYLI	Queen's Own Yorkshire Light Infantry
RAMC	Royal Army Medical Corps
RFA	Royal Field Artillery
RHA	Royal Horse Artillery
RGA	Royal Garrison Artillery
RMA	Royal Marine Artillery
RME	Royal Marine Engineers
RMLI	Royal Marine Light Infantry
RMP	Royal Military Police
RFC	Royal Flying Corps
RIR	Royal Irish Rifles
RAC	Royal Armoured Corps
RTR	Royal Tank Regiment
SBP	Shoulder Belt Plate
TA	Territorial Army
Vol.	Volunteer
Vic R or VR	Queen Victoria
w/m	white metal
b/m	bi-metal
WWI	World War One (1914–19)
WWII	World War Two (1939–45)
WO	warrant officer

This list is by no means complete and does not include such regiments as the REs or RA (Royal Engineers, Royal Artillery), whose initials are well-known.

If your collection is to be based on a general hotchpotch of badges then without exceptional luck, you will need plenty of patience, room and time and may have to wait a lifetime to fill one particular space. It is far better, therefore, to adopt a more limited plan of campaign opting for regiments that participated in, say, the Boer War and World War 1, or saw action during World War 2. One of my clients set his sights on accumulating all the London regiments of the Great War while another hit upon the idea of collecting only insignia of Cavalry, Hussars and Dragoons.

33. Scottish regimental bonnet badges. *Left to right:* Cameron Highlanders; King's Own Scottish Borderers; Highland Light Infantry

Once you have set your sights, it is as well to remember the variations one will encounter. It is not enough just to collect a badge, clean it and pack it away in a tray; try to learn something about its history and the different patterns that were issued. The Cambridgeshire Regiment, for example, issued two different badges. One title is spelt Cambridgeshire and the other Cambridgshire, the latter being the rarity. A Royal Inniskilling Fusilier badge exists in three types. The first is a brass grenade with a w/m Castle of Enniskillen and a St George's flag flying to the left. A second badge was issued about 1926 when the grenade motif was discarded in favour of the Castle, solitary, with 'Inniskilling' scroll and flag flying to the right. In 1934 the original grenade badge was reintroduced but this time the flag hung to the right. About 1940 a fresh batch of these badges appeared bearing a mis-spelt 'Inneskilling'. The badge of the Royal Artillery has alternatively a 'running-wheel', a w/m and laurel spray in a scroll or a version with 'Volunteers' in the scroll. Indeed, so many variations exist that one would require a book on the subject of badges alone (such a one is *Military Badge Collecting* by John Gaynor). All of them go to make up a collection, and the collector should consider every known example if it comes within his own particular range of badges.

Even minor discrepancies make a badge well worth collecting. Details may vary only slightly; on the bonnet badge of the Argyll & Sutherland Highlanders, the wild cat can be found with its tail raised, tail curled around its feet, its head facing the viewer or facing front.

Some idea of the different types to be encountered is given by this list.

Royal Scots: Available in all-brass and one in bi-metal (b/m).

Fife and Forfar Yeomanry: In all-brass and one in b/m.

Middlesex Regt.: One in all-brass, another in b/m, and a third b/m that bears the battle honour of the Boer War 'South Africa 1900–02' (worn by 7th, 8th, 9th

Battalions. Tenth had honour scroll left blank.) A rarity has Public Works Pioneer Battalion beneath title scroll.

Essex Regt.: In b/m with regimental castle; flag and large central tower (pre-1900). in b/m, no flag, with three towers. 4th, 5th, 6th, 7th Battalions wore same badge with the Sphinx's plinth left blank and 'South Africa 1900–02' in scroll beneath title.

Army Service Corps.: This corps boasts three variations; one with a filled centre, one void, and another with a much wider, fuller centre wreath.

Gloucestershire Regt.: Unique as they wear two cap badges; a large Sphinx on a tablet 'Egypt', and a small ($\frac{1}{2}$in) circular badge worn on the back of the head-dress. This back-badge was to commemorate a back-to-back stand against the French at the Battle of Alexandria.

Suffolk Regt.: This regiment has had about six different badges ranging from one in all-brass, b/m, and officer's bronze. A selection of 'Gibraltar Castles' can be found. The scarce badge which was struck without the *Mantis Insignia Calpe* inscription is well worth searching for.

28th Battalion Artists Rifles: Two badges; one with 'Artists' scroll was struck in black, brass and w/m. Another pattern struck in brass as well as w/m carried 'Artists Rifles' on the scroll. The twin heads portray Mars, the God of War, and Minerva, Goddess of the Arts.

The list of interesting, eminently collectable bonnet badges, piper's badges, badges for nco's and officers, badges issued to Commonwealth troops during the two world wars is almost endless as is the fascination which the history of these badges will provoke in the average collector.

Since 1953 and the introduction of the anodised aluminium (a/a) cap badge, some inveterate collectors have steadfastly refused to countenance any of these glittering trinkets in their collection. I feel some sympathy with them, but this horrific innovation, the 'Staybrite' badge (introduced into the Services to obviate cleaning) must be included in any collection that pretends to being an unbroken series. Apoplexy more extreme still is caused by the mention of the wartime plastic badge. Manufactured in 1941, the plastic badge was introduced as part of a drive to conserve vital metals. It came in brown, grey and, in some instances, black. They were never very popular with servicemen, and collectors shy away from them like the plague. Crude in design and unattractive in appearance, they are an unsightly reminder of the privations which countries at war voluntarily suffer.

Having covered or, rather, uncovered most of the snags and pitfalls in the path of the novice, it is, however, necessary to say something about helmet plates and helmet plate centres (HPs & HPCs). HPs were worn on the old blue-cloth spiked helmet which was shaped very much like the British police helmet. They were also worn on the brass and w/m Yeomanry helmet which was common at the turn of the century. Most HPs were made in two and, sometimes, three sections, so allowing the HPC to be removed if the need arose. A large back-plate in the form of a 'Brunswick Star' was screwed to the helmet, while the centre was held in place with four brass pins or pieces of wash leather. Later, as the helmet fell by the wayside giving place to soft side cap and stiff-peaked SD cap, these HPCs seemed to have been issued with a slide-fastener instead of the four loops. The example of a West Yorkshire Regiment badge has just the slide with no sign whatsoever of the four loops having ever been fitted. It is thought that these badges were worn in the twisted folds of the pagri so very popular with British troops stationed in India during World War 1.

Whilst on the subject of large badges, remember that many cross-belt, sabretache or pouch badges resemble the larger Glengarry Grenades and Fusilier fur-cap badges. It is not too difficult to distinguish between them, since the former are usually fitted with a set of threaded brass screws, while the cap badges have three or four small copper loops (very much like those fitted to a collar-dog). Occasionally these threaded sections are lopped off and the badge is then offered as a genuine cap piece. Close examination should soon uncover that ruse.

As your collection grows and you begin to meet fellow collectors it will soon become apparent that no two collectors are the same. Some will specialise in HPCs while others will stick to cap badges of certain regiments. Others take plunder indiscriminately; HPs, badges, collar-dogs, shoulder titles and buttons, indeed, almost anything that has a military flavour. There is, however, something to be said for specialising in military buttons. Apart from being relatively cheap, they do not take up all that much room; a dozen or so cards of mounted buttons in a small office drawer will act as a discreet display case for 300 choice examples.

As with much militaria, buttons have a venerable history. The army of Elizabeth I were buttoned although these early examples tended to be more armorial than

34. Pugri badge of West Yorkshire Regiment – note the extra long slide

regimental in design. These hand-made articles came in all manner of materials from horn to ivory, silver, tin and even gold – depending upon the wealth and fancy of the regiment's colonel-in-chief. The advent of the New Model Army in 1666 saw the introduction of regimental buttons proper, but, even so, these varied in size and the materials of which they were made.

Dating British buttons is a fairly easy and straightforward task. One can discover the period of manufacture by studying the different types of shank and style of actual title; it was not until about 1767 that the War Office ordered that the regimental numbering which had been allotted to the infantry in 1751 was to be embossed on the buttons worn by all ranks. Although a general overhaul in the design of buttons followed, it was well after 1850 before the common pewter button was finally replaced by the familiar brass one.

The leading military button-makers are two old-established firms, Jennen's and Firmin's. Since these firms underwent various changes of title, it is possible to date the successive stages of their companies accurately, Messrs Jennen and Co (1800–32); Charles Jennen (1832–1912); Jennen and Co, London (1912–24). The firm amalgamated in 1924 with Messrs Gaunt and Sons, of Birmingham and London. Firmin's history is more complex: Thomas Firmin (1677); Firmin (1770); Samuel Firmin (1771–80); Firmin & Westall (1797–80); Phillip Firmin (1812); Firmin & Longdale (1815); Firmin & Sons (1824); Robert Firmin (1826); Firmin & King (1839); Phillip & Samuel Firmin (1841); Firmin & Sons Ltd, as they have remained until the present day.

Only in 1855 did the button as we know it today really arrive, as, with the introduction of the tunic, new and larger buttons became the order of the day. However change then, as ever, was not universal. Officers still preferred to retain the old ways

35. Selection of British pre-1953 regimental buttons. *Top row (left to right):* Royal Artillery; Royal Army Ordnance Corps; Royal Army Medical Corps; Royal Army Pay Corps (1929 on); *bottom row:* West Yorkshire Regt.; Tank Corps (1917–23); South Staffordshire Regt.; Corps of Royal Military Police (George VI)

36. Selection of shoulder-titles and collar dogs. *Top row (left to right):* Essex Yeomanry; Royal Horse Artillery; *middle row:* Essex Yeomanry; Essex Regt.; Queen's Own Hussars; *bottom row:* Army Service Corps. As a point of interest the Queen's Own Hussars badge also saw service as a beret badge!

and continued to sport buttons of horn, gold and silver. Right up until the Boer War they sported these bright and shiny buttons – until they encountered the accurate rifles of 'Johnny Kruger'. Contemporary reports often tell of young officers being hit dead-centre on their middle tunic button. Orders were finally issued for the wearing of khaki, and officers' buttons can be found in wood, leather and a rather strange gutta-percha mixture. I have found one example of the latter which bears the insignia of the City Imperial Volunteers.

Copies of old buttons do exist and it would be incorrect to class these as forgeries. Some officers' and other ranks' buttons of 1855–71 have been restruck from time to time either for regimental or private collections. These sometimes bear the name of the manufacturing firm or perhaps the words 'Special Made'.

Buttons that have served a double purpose are also to be found; relics of a lost world of espionage and military intrigue. During the Franco–Prussian War, messages were concealed inside uniform buttons and flown out of beleaguered Paris in observation balloons. In both the world wars buttons have been used to carry maps, microfilm and cyphers. An innocent-looking collar stud worn by the RAF concealed a tiny compass. Scraping off the thin layer of enamel revealed a small glass cover with vital works beneath. This was intended to help those flyers who had been shot down over enemy territory.

Closely allied with cap badges and regimental buttons are collar-dogs. Originally about the same size as a cap badge they have, over the years, been reduced to make a far neater piece of insignia. At first sight, some of these miniature badges could be mistaken for a cap badge. (Some Lancer regiments still use a collar-dog as a cap badge, as did the old Rough Riders.) However, one soon begins to identify one from the other. A general guideline is that collar-dogs are not only smaller, but also boast a pair of copper fixing loops instead of the brass slide-fastener. This generalisation, like all others, may be confounded by the odd badge which was manufactured with both slide and loop fitting.

Some collectors never purchase a badge or collar-dog which has either a missing slide or damaged loops. By and large, this is a wise way of collecting. Who wants tray-loads of battered, mutilated examples? However, confronted with the chance of acquiring a rare Royal Naval Air Service, Armoured Car Division collar badge with both loops missing even if this is not strictly a collar-dog (being one of the pair of oval, bronzed insignia being worn on the lapels of a naval jacket), then such rigidity would be foolish. If it's a rare example, snap it up and hope eventually to come across one in original condition. Rarities exist, and generally speaking a rare cap badge means a rare collar-dog.

In some instances, slides and loops are soldered back on. This is a rather tricky task and one that takes some practice, but for those with a suitable soldering iron, a steady hand and a little know-how a very worthwhile one. If you do try your hand with this restoration work it is best to use brass slide-fasteners taken from fairly common badges such as RA, RE, RAOC. Resist above all the habit of one old gentleman of my acquaintance who, finding that badges wouldn't lie flat on his velvet-lined trays, promptly chopped off all loops and slides.

Part and parcel of this particular field of collection are brass shoulder titles. These prove a rather complex hobby; many of these titles sport only a few obscure letters and numbers. The list of abbreviations in this chapter should help to decode them, but, should you stumble across any obscure examples, then a reply-paid letter to the Imperial War Museum should provide the answer.

A hitherto unmined area of militaria is the cloth square worn on battle-dress sleeves, known officially as the formation badge (or, more familiarly, the 'Div-Sign'). (Read *Formation Badges of World War 2* by Lieutenant-Colonel Howard N. Cole [Arms and Armour Press].) Originally introduced during World War 1, they were readopted in 1940. A variety of designs were used and many owe their existence to local legend or an historical link. Cleaned and pressed, they make an interesting and unusual collection, and, like the early days of cap-badge collecting, are still fairly reasonable in price.

Cleaning and presentation largely depend on how much room you wish to devote to the collection. Mounting them in glazed picture frames is all very fine if the room is large enough, but it can be a little imposing to be constantly under the gaze of what should be a hobby not a chore. Indeed, cleaning should only be carried out if the badges are suffering badly from verdigris or heavy staining. In chronic cases of verdigris, it is advisable to leave the affected badge soaking in a neat solution of lemon juice. Brushing well with an old toothbrush will soon remove the offensive green deposit and a wash in warm, soapy water will quickly neutralise the acid. Staining can also be removed in the same way, but it may be enough to give the metal a brush with a brass-bristled suede brush. Steer clear of abrasives; metal polishes such as Brasso or Duraglit may be good enough for brass-hilted bayonets and swords, or brass and copper powder flasks, but these cleaners tend to leave a deposit of filth in the fine relief work of badges. Of course back in the days of army 'bull-shine', it was the done thing to burnish badges and brass-work to a fine old state. The results of this zealousness are now little more than polished pieces of metal. All one can do with these is to polish them lightly with a wadding cleaner, and brush out any residue from the crevices.

Some collectors treat their badges with a clear shellac, such as Joy's Transparent Lacquer, after cleaning. This is ideal for those who live where the briny air plays havoc with metal. However, central heating and pollution cause noticeable changes on this protective coating of shellac. The metal beneath becoming discoloured after a few years.

Bronze or bronzed insignia should not be cleaned at all. If the badge or button seems to be clogged or coated with a layer of dirt, a light application of machine oil should be rubbed gently over it and then removed with a soft cloth. Silver items (officers only!) can be silver-dipped, washed and then polished with a suitable cloth.

To display a collection of badges, buttons, collar-dogs or shoulder titles, one can, as I have already pointed out, mount them in picture frames. Another method is to mount them on velvet or cloth-covered cardboard trays. Holes can be punched or cut in the cards allowing the slide or loops to be pushed through. These cards can then be stowed away in drawer, cupboard or filing cabinet, discreetly awaiting the discerning and admiring eye of the enthusiast – even if it is only that of the collection's proud owner!

5 European and Oriental Armour

Nobody knows for sure when the use of body armour became a standard practice. We find ancient references to jackets stuffed with wool or hair and, in other instances, coats being covered with chain scales or metal plates. Foot soldiers of Ancient Egypt carried large shields which not only acted as a protection for their body in battle but also as a kind of palisade when stuck into the ground in front of entrenched troops. Later, the shield was not protection enough, for their simple loin cloths gave way to tunics, leather breast-plates and mantles covered with bronze scales, these last being introduced after the capture of similar armour worn by the King of Syria when Thutmosis I swept down on that country in 1530 BC.

The earliest painting depicting scale armour was found in the tomb of Kenamon, who lived in Egypt during the reign of Amenhotep II (1436–1411 BC). This painting is of a jacket covered in bronze scales, with a high leather collar. Another wall painting, this time in the tomb of Rameses III (1198–1167 BC) shows a long coat completely covered (even the neck and short sleeves) with interlaced bronze scales. Over the centuries, archaeological digs have unearthed fragments of scale armour that once belonged to proud warrior nations such as the Scythians, Avars and Sarmatians.

Oriental armour has changed very little since those ancient times and as late as 1900 with the Third China War, warriors met the invading 'foreign dogs' garbed in armour and brandishing cross-bows, bills and lances.

From the beginning of the Christian period right through to the eleventh century, European armour changed very little. Church brasses and effigies give a good idea of how those knights of old dressed to kill. With the introduction of plate armour, a warrior was hard pressed to do anything but be helped up onto the back of his heavy war-horse, take his mace or sword, and trot off in the general direction of the enemy. If he was unfortunate enough to become unhorsed, then he lay where he had fallen, helpless as an unpended turtle and just as vulnerably exposed to the predations of passing foot soldiers. So absurd were the limitations placed on the wearer that King James I once remarked in ironic praise that 'It not only protected the wearer, but also prevented him from injuring any other person'. During the Crusades, a very

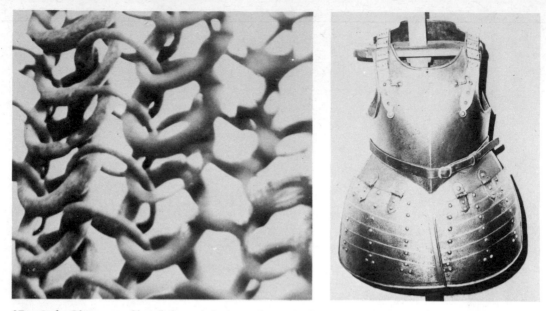

37. *Left:* Close-up of hand-forged chain mail attached to 18th century Indo-Persian *Kulah-Khud*. 38. *Right:* Back and breast-plate of mid-seventeenth century armour bearing the armourer's proof marks

popular form of light armour was the hauberk, a tunic or long coat of chain mail. This mail coat was in use from the eleventh until well into the fourteenth century.

Regulations for the care and attention of arms and armour were rigorous. So that a body of men might always be ready to take to the field of battle, a law was enacted by Henry II in AD 1181. There was a further corroboration of this law, known as the Statute of Winchester, during the reign of Edward I. Under this law, every man was bound to provide and keep arms and armour, according to his estate or goods. The armour and weapons were allotted as follows:

'Every one possessed of lands to the yearly value of fifteen pounds, and forty marks in goods, to keep a haubergeon, an iron headpiece, a sword, knife, and horse. Those having from ten and under fifteen pounds in lands and chattels, or the value of forty marks, the same as the preceding class, the horse excepted. Persons having an hundred shillings per annum in land, and upwards, were to keep a doublet, a headpiece of iron, a sword, and a knife. And from forty shillings annual rent in land, and upwards, to one hundred, a sword, bow and arrows, and a knife. A review of these arms was to be made twice a year, by two constables out of every hundred, who were to report defaulters to the justices, and they were to present them to the King in parliament.'

By an act of 1588, those temporal persons, having estates of a thousand pounds or upwards, should keep to hand:

39.   Close-up of armourer's mark 'T.R.' and proof

'Six horses or geldings fit for mounting demi-launces, three at least to have sufficient harness, steel saddles and weapons. Ten light horses or geldings, with the weapons and harness requisite for light-horsemen; also forty corselets furnished [i.e. completely furnished with head-piece, gorget, back and breast plate, and iron tasses], forty almaine rivetts, or instead of the said forty almaine rivetts, forty coats of plate, corselets or brigandines furnished; forty pikes, thirty long bowes, thirty sheafs of arrows [a sheaf contained twenty-four arrows], thirty steele cappes or sculles, twenty black bill or halberts, twenty haquebuts [a handgun called a hook-butt], and twenty morians or sallets.

'No man shall carry arms out of the kingdom, unless by the command of our Lord the King, nor shall any man sell arms to another, who means to carry them out of the kingdom.

'No Jew shall have in his custody a coat of mail or habergeon, but shall sell or give it away, or in some other manner so dispose of it, that it shall remain in the King's service.'

With the introduction of the rifled 'gonne', plate armour became increasingly thick and heavy. It was not enough for an armourer to proof his work against the onslaught of mace, sword, lance and cross-bow bolt. Now he had to satisfy his master that his bespoke iron-suit would stand up to a spinning rifle ball. Close study of armour in our museums will show the presence of a number of small dents – nine times out of ten, these will be proof-marks. This blanket obligation to provide

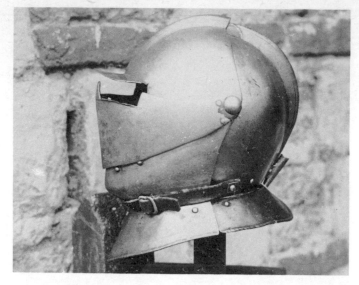

40. Close-helmet of the mid-seventeenth century, in very good order and well-preserved

armour produced some bizarre variations. Those who could not afford a heavy suit of armour might apparently hang small anvils about their bodies to guard against harquebuss fire.[1] At the battle of Fornoue, a party of Charles VIII's Italian knights, having been overthrown, could not be slain because of the thickness of their armour. Instead, they had to be broken up like huge lobsters with large wood-cutter's axes.

Collecting armour is not a poor man's hobby or pastime. A full suit of *reproduction* armour will cost about two hundred pounds, while a nineteenth-century piece, very popular with monied Victorians, and usually made in France, Germany or Spain, will fetch between seven and nine hundred pounds under the hammer. A genuine, fully authenticated suit would fetch upwards of two thousand pounds.

Don't rush into buying the first suit or piece that is offered you. Armour is very hard to find and even single gauntlets don't come onto the market every day. Take your time, ask questions, and take that knowledgeable friend along just to be safe. It is very difficult to distinguish between fourteenth-, fifteenth- and sixteenth-century armour unless you know your subject. Some suits may have been 'married up' at a later date, and, in some instances, good repair work by a blacksmith may have been carried out in the seventeenth and eighteenth centuries.

With modern reproductions, our 'armourer' will probably have used the modern gas welding to forge each special piece. It will pay you to look for the burn marks which often rise to the surface after completion. On a genuine piece of armour these burn marks will have dispersed with the passing of time.

Cleaning and preservation of old armour is always a difficult task and should be approached with some care. Heavily rusted plate armour should be tackled by hand and not with a power drill and wire brush. That is all right for the expert who knows just how much pressure to apply when using such a powerful tool. At first the novice should be content to use wire-wool and oil and perhaps just a fine piece of wet-and-dry emery paper. At the most he should only resort to the use of a hand wire brush to take off the stubborn layer of congealed rust. Once the rust is removed and the bare metal is revealed, then care should be exercised to make sure that any proof-marks are not damaged with further excessive cleaning. For the final finish it is advisable to heat the metal gently, thus removing excessive moisture, and then cover all parts with a liberal application of machine or sperm oil. Clear varnish as a protective covering is not advisable; any trapped moisture tends to rise to the surface after a month or two. Leather strappings should be treated with saddle soap.

Terms used with Armour
EUROPEAN TERMS

ALLETTES	In armour plates, usually rectangular, of metal or leather covered with cloth or other light material, fastened by a lace to the back or side of the shoulders, they commonly display armorial bearings; worn *c* 1275 to *c* 1325.
ARMING DOUBLET	Sleeved coat worn under armour; fifteenth and sixteenth century.
ARMING POINTS	Laces for attaching parts of armour together.
AKETON	Defensive body armour composed of numerous folds of linen stuffed with cotton, wool or hair, quilted and covered with leather or doe skin.
BASSINET OR BASCINET	Light steel helmet worn with camail, sometimes fitted with a visor. Worn by most English infantry during the reigns of Edward II, III, and Richard II, they were usually sported on the outskirts of a battle.
BESAGUES	Small plates worn in front of the armpits.
BEVOR	Plate defence for chin and throat.
BRASSART	Plate armour defence for the arm.
BRIGANDINE	Aptly named after soldiers who combined plunder with fighting. A coat of quilted cloth made in the form of a doublet lined with canvas, with rows of metal plates fastened by rivets.
BUFF COAT	Coat of heavy leather.
BURGONET	A helmet thought to have been invented by the Burgundians and constructed in the form of a human head.
CAMAIL	Hood of chain mail; first worn attached to the hauberk, then separated from it with tippet of mail over shoulders, and in the fourteenth century attached to bassinet.

Fig. 6   Full suit
of Armour (*c.* 1540):
A – crest,
B – skull,
C – visor,
D – bevor,
 E – gorget,
 F – haute-piece,
G – pauldron,
H – couter,
 I – vambrace,
 J – chain-mail shirt or fald,
K – gauntlet,
 L – cuishe,
M – poleyn,
N – greave,
O – sabaton

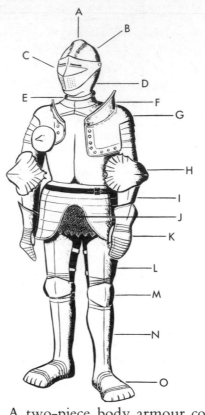

CUIRASS	A two-piece body armour consisting of a back- and breast-plate held in position by straps and buckles. Originally made from hard leather but can also be found in brass and light steel. Worn by most armies well into the nineteenth century, while in France was still in vogue up to World War 1.
CABACETE	A Spanish term for a morion helmet having a narrow brim.
CHAUSSES	Leg defences of mail.
DEMI-BRASSART	Plate defence for outside of arm.
GADLINGS	Spikes or knobs on plate gauntlets.
GAMBESON	Garment of padded cloth worn under hauberk or as sole defence.
GIPON	Close-fitting vest of cloth, worn over armour. *c* 1350–1410.
GORGET	Piece of neck armour which linked the helmet to breast-plate protecting the neck from a direct blow. Made in

iron, steel or brass. This piece can claim the distinction of being the last portion of armour to be worn. In the British Army it finished its day as a small silver or gilt badge suspended from chains or a ribbon, but in other countries it still plays an important part in the equipment of the standard bearer.

GUSSETS	Pieces of flexible armour fitted between the gaps of plate defences.
GAUNTLETS	Sometimes made from chain mail, or small plates of iron riveted together to form an articulated glove in the form of a lobster's tail.
HAKETON	Studded, stiffened or quilted body defence, of cloth, leather and metal, with moderately long skirts.
HAUBERK	Shirt of chain or other mail.
HELM	Complete barrel or dome-shaped head defence of plate.
HUFKEN	Thought to be a light head-piece worn by archers during the reign of Elizabeth I.
JAZERINE	Armour of small plates laced on leather or cloth.
LORICA	Body armour worn by Romans.
LAMELLAE	Small plates of leather, metal, bone or wood used in the construction of lamellar armour.
MAIL SKIRT	Skirt of chain mail worn under taces and tuiles.
MAIL STANDARD	Collar of chain mail.
NASAL-BAR	A form of face defence attached to the front of a helmet. On European helmets the bar could sometimes be lifted up and over the top of the helmet, while Oriental warriors preferred a sliding method or a plain fixture.
PANACHE	A plume or bush of feathers worn on the helm.
POULDRON	Plate defence for the shoulders.
POT	Very much akin to a morian but with a broad brim.
POURPOINT	A body defence of cloth or leather, padded or quilted.
REREBRACE	Plate or leather defence for upper arm.
SABATONS OR SOLLERETS	Articulated plate defences for the feet.
SALADE, SALLET OR CELATE	Light helmet worn without a crest and sometimes with a visor. A manuscript inventory of equipment found in different arsenals and garrisons during Edward VI's reign (1547–53) lists: 'At Hampton Court sallet for archers on horseback, sallets with grates, and old sallets with vizards; at Windsor, sallets and skull; at Calais, sallet with vysars and beavers'.

SCULL	A light helmet in the shape of a basin or bowl and worn by English cavalry well into the last quarter of the eighteenth century.
SPURS — PRICK	In form of plain goad; early form.
SPURS — ROWEL	With spiked wheel; later form.
SURCOAT	Coat, usually sleeveless, worn over armour.
TABARD	Short loose surcoat, open at sides, with short tab-like sleeves, sometimes worn with armour, and emblazoned with arms; distinctive garment of heralds.
TACES OR TONLETS	Articulated defences for hips and lower part of body.
TUILES	Plates attached to and hanging from the edge of taces or tonlets.
VAMBRACE	Plate defence for lower arm.
VAMPLATE	Funnel-shaped hand-guard of lance.
VIZOR	Hinged face-guard of bascinet, salade, close helmet etc.

HORSE ARMOUR

CHAMFRON	Head armour mainly worn by heavy war-horses and made from leather, iron, copper or brass, or even silver studded with gems. A large spike or horn sometimes protruded from the centre of the forehead. Although greatly sought after, prudence should be exercised, as first-class reproductions are being manufactured. A chamfron reaching only to the middle of the face is known as a demi-chamfron. Closely linked to these is the crinière, or manefaire, made up of a number of small metal plates clipped together and hooked to the chamfron, thus forming a flexible neck armour.
CRUPPER	Armour formed from leather, copper, iron or brass, worn over the buttocks and descending down to the hocks.
FLANCHARD	A defence for a horse's flank usually suspended from the saddle.
POITRINAL OR PECTORAL	Plates of metal rivetted together to form armour for breast and shoulder of the horse.

JAPANESE TERMS

Akoda-nari	A form of ridged helmet-bowl.
Ashigaru-gusoku	Foot soldier's armour.
Bajo-date	Horseman's shield.

94

Ba–men	A chamfron.
Biobu–date	A folding shield.
Dō	Cuirass.
Eboshi–nari	Tall cap-shaped helmet.
Gusoku	A complete suit of armour.
Habaki	Form of leggings.
Haidate	Armour for thighs, tied around the waist.
Hambō	Face defence.
Hiza–yoroi	Early form of leg and thigh armour.
Ita–mono	Armour made from single piece of leather or iron.
Jingasa	War-cap of leather, iron, copper or even paper.
Kashira–date	Helmet crest.
Kusari	Mail.
Kusari–katabira	A coat of mail lined with cloth or silk.
Mitsu–kuwagata	Set of horns worn on the front of a helmet.
Muna–ita	Breast-plate.
Neri–gawa	Hard leather.
Nodowa	A type of gorget.
Ō–sode	Shoulderguards.
Sane–yoroi	A form of lamellar armour
Sawari	White armour – a rather unusual method of plating iron with white metal.
Sode	Defence for upper arm and shoulder.
Suneate	Shinguards.
Tameshi	Proofing armour with musket balls or lances.
Uma–yoroi	Horse armour.
Yoroi	A form of armour.
Yoroi no karabitsu	Special kind of chest for storing armour.

CHINESE TERMS

Jên ma k'ai	Special type of horse armour.
Koa	Quilted coat armour.
Kia	Leather armour.
Kiai	Horse armour of leather scales.
Lien so kia	Chain mail armour.
Pei k'uei	Round shield of hide.
Si lin kia	Armour formed from thin iron scales or plates.

PERSIAN TERMS

Bazuband	Plate armour for the forearm.

Kūiris	Form of camail attached to the base of a helmet.
Kulah-khud	Helmet.
Sipar	Shield.
Zirih-baktah	Coat of mail.

INDIAN TERMS

Bagta-kalghi	Plume of feathers worn on a helmet.
Baktar-zillo	A form of scale armour.
Bhanjce	Armoured coat complete with gorget.
Chakra	A sharpened steel quoit used as a throwing weapon.
Char-aina	A form of cuirass constructed from four plates.
Chihal'ta Hazar Māshā	A coat consisting of many layers of cloth covered with silk and studded with thousands of tiny, gilt nails.
Dastana	Plate defences for the forearm.
Dhal	A shield.
Gardani	Neck armour for a horse.
G'hug'hwah	Coat of mail with hood attached.
Kajam	Mail armour for a horse.
Kant'hah sobha	Gorget.
Kashka	Chamfron for horse.
Kubega	Type of quilted coat worn under mail.
Kukri	The famous Gurkha knife.
Tōp	A helmet of either mail or metal.
Zirih	A shirt of mail.

6 Swords Daggers and Bayonets

Visit any museum of note or study the many graphic prints and paintings left by our war-hungry forbears and one can soon establish that swords and daggers of some description have been with us for a great number of years.

Although they cannot claim to be the oldest of weapons (stone axes and clubs claiming this accolade), swords have been wielded from about 3000 BC. Before this, we find fine flint examples with long slim, finely knapped blades quite capable of disembowelling man or beast. Metal-edged swords can be traced back to ancient Egypt where several types of blades were employed. Greek swords were basically a slashing weapon but the *gladius* sported by invading Roman legionaries was strictly a stabbing weapon. Behind a phalanx of rigid shields, a legionary, protected by iron-plated breast-plate, helmet with cheek-pieces, armed with short-sword, barbed javelin (for *hastati* and *principes*), pike (for *trarii*) and dressed in cloth breeches, short-sleeved tunic and sandals, could manipulate the short but heavy, double-edged weapon with deadly efficiency. The two or three inches of blade protruding around the side of the shield could be thrust into an enemy's exposed belly.

To give some little idea of the fighting strength of a Roman army, a *phalanx* was formed of 4,096 men in sixteen ranks of 256 and a legion consisted of 4,200–6,000 men in three ranks.

Although reliable facts about the manufacture and usage of swords are hard to come by until the late seventeenth century, we do have a fair idea of the types of weapons carried by knights of the medieval period. The sword of that age was designed primarily as an offensive weapon, having a single cross or quillon as a hand guard which was sometimes straight and sometimes swept up or down. The blade was usually straight with a double edge, and the grip or hilt made of wood, covered in fish skin or leather and sometimes bound with cord or gold and silver wire. To balance the long blade (26–40 in *c* 1252, 46–56 in later), a knob of shaped metal known as a pommel was fitted to the top of the hilt. The shape of this pommel helps to determine the age of a medieval sword and further information can be gleaned from a very useful work *The Archaeology of Weapons* by R. E. Oakeshott.

All through the Middle Ages the sword was designed solely as a cutting weapon

Fig. 7 Hilt of rapier, *c.* 1560: A – blade,
B – ports or side-rings, C – ricasso, D – arms
of hilt, E – diagonal counter-guards,
F – quillons, G – quillon block, H – grip,
I – knuckle-guard or bow, J – pommel,
L – button

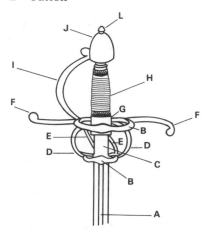

41.   *Right:* Mid-seventeenth century bronze
hilted sword. The single-edge flamboyant
blade bears the running-wolf mark of
Solingen. This specimen was discovered in the
attic of a house in the Essex town of Colchester

with a flat, broad blade and single, well-honed edge. With the advent of heavy plate armour the need for a more robust thrusting weapon became apparent, not so much pierce armour as to slice through chain mail and heavy leather doublets. Originally designed to be carried on horseback and used single-handed the hand-and-a-half sword enabled the combatant to swing the heavy blade with both hands.

Sword collectors must be prepared to keep an open mind in determining a country of origin. Over the centuries, most leading blade manufacturers were situated in Cologne, Poitou, Passau, Pavia, Valencia, Solingen and Bordeaux, while blades from Toledo and Toloseta were reckoned to be the finest in the world. It is believed that a secret chemical property found in the turbulent waters of the river Tagus which surrounds Toledo on three sides, greatly enhanced the forging and tempering process, giving a hardness and cutting edge comparable only with those blades forged in ancient Japan.

As with all worthwhile objects, especially weapons, inferior copies were made with great detail being given to prominent cutler's and armourer's marks. Blades were often sold in bulk, shipped to a customer, stowed away in barrels of wine – there was, at one time, a tax levied on blades imported into England – and hilts were eventually added by local swordsmiths to order. With this haphazardness of origin, one is apt to think that one has purchased a rare Juan Martinez blade topped with a Scottish basket hilt when the chances are that it is a contemporary, but nevertheless interesting, copy.

Not many medieval swords remain available now for the average collector so it is advisable to make a study of those in the museums just in case one is lucky enough to have such a treasured item thrust in one's way. One or two fine examples are still in service, being carried in stately ceremonies at such places as York (hand-and-a-half sword of the Emperor Sigismund 1410–38), and the City of Bristol (famous Pearl sword *c.* 1400).

During the late fourteenth and early fifteenth centuries, the offensive arms of a horseman, or man-at-arms, were a sword or swords, a lance and a small dagger, known as a misericorde. Knights frequently carried two swords, one in a belt at their side and the other tied to their saddle-bow. In the *Speculum Regale*, written about the twelfth century, among other directions for the arming of a horseman, are these: 'Let him have two swords, one in his belt and the other hanging to his saddle-bowe, with a war knife.' Men-at-arms also frequently carried iron maces, suspended from their saddle-bows. Archers were known to sport heavy lead mallets which they used with great gusto to unhorse galloping enemy horsemen. The misericorde was so called either because it was mercifully used in putting out of their misery the desperately wounded, or, from the sight of it, was apt to cause helpless victims to call out 'Misericorde' – mercy or quarter. It was indeed a fearsome weapon, being designed to cut through the leather or mail defences protecting either the neck or armpits. A rather unusual Italian version was furnished with a pair of spring-loaded blades. Once the point had been thrust into the yielding flesh, a slight touch of a concealed button would send the sharpened segments flashing out and upwards, thus extending the wound some three inches on either side.

The chances of finding an early sword still complete with original scabbard are very slim. The ravages of time and our climate soon reduce the thin wood and leather or velvet covering to dust. Even a scabbard of, say, a hundred years ago is slowly cracking and crumbling away with each passing year. Yet another factor, which destroys much of the fine etched or engraved detail on a blade, is the curse of 'poisoned finger'. As we have already mentioned, acid or rust marks caused by sweaty fingers on a gun barrel are not irremovable *if* you act early enough. On a sword or dagger blade, however, the damage is often only discovered very much later. Once the steel has been returned to its scabbard or sheath, the corrosive effects of 'poisoned fingers' can work away undisturbed and undetected. When you've had a visitor looking over your collection, it is always advisable to give each blade a quick wipe-over with an oily cloth. This not only removes finger marks but also prevents rusting.

The novice is advised to concentrate on the swords and daggers of the eighteenth

42. Heavy fighting *Kindjal* from the Caucasus. Weapons of this type were carried by warriors of Persia, Russia and the Balkans

43 Sword of a Knight of Pythias, a U.S. masonic order founded in 1864. It has a brass scabbard and furniture

and nineteenth centuries. Here one will find a vast array of weapons ranging from those carried by officers in the East India Company to a General Officer's sabre with 'Mameluke' hilt pattern of 1831. The latter sword has an ivory grip, curved single-edged blade 30in long, and is carried in a gilt-brass sheath. This weapon is now greatly sought after and commands a high price.

From Spain, the States (Confederate and Yankee), France, Denmark, Prussia, Sweden and Britain, have come over 150 different types and patterns to pick from. Really good swords might be a fine example wielded by the Old Guard of Napoleon, the *Claidheamh mor* or Claymore of the wild Scot, or the beautifully made Samurai sword, so sharp that, in the right hands, it is capable of cutting a man in half with a single blow. If you decide to collect handsome or pretty swords, you could specialise in the ornate and finely executed levée officers' swords of the late eighteenth or early nineteenth century. These weapons are beautiful examples of British craftmanship, being blued and embossed with battle honours or regimental history. Another type of blade in this category is the naval officer's dress sword, which has a gilt hilt and scabbard fittings and usually has sailing ships and other naval motifs embossed or engraved on the blade. Swords bearing the stamp 'CSA' (Confederate States Army) are rather scarce and form an interesting part of American military history.

Where can these swords be bought? No longer do we find that umbrella stand or old World War 1 shell case crammed tight with edged weapons, standing in a junk-shop corner. If we do glimpse the odd hilt or two from time to time in these havens of junk, then the chances are that they are nothing more than Indian Bazaar rubbish, shipped over to Britain within the last ten years as glitter-swag for bingo halls or cheap seaside gift shops. Look closely on the roughly forged blade (old car springs in the main), and sometimes you will see, weakly etched, Made in India.

Specialist auctioneers (those listed in Chapter IV) will prove very helpful although it is advisable to pay a visit to view the goods offered. Even auctioneers are human and can easily make mistakes. If you don't feel confident enough to draw your own conclusions or make a bid, then consult one of the dealers who provide a buying service. If you do attend an auction with your eye on a particular piece, then follow the immemorial rule of most dealers – mark your catalogue in advance with the maximum figure you intend to pay for each item. It is all too easy to be swept along on a wave of bidding and to end up paying well over the odds for an ordinary piece of merchandise.

BAYONETS

Closely allied with swords and daggers is the ever popular bayonet. To be found all over the world, most nineteenth and twentieth century armies have sported a bayonet of some sort. If you remain sceptical, bewilder yourself with the variety in *The Collector's Pictorial Book of Bayonets* by Frederick J. Stephens. The evolution of the bayonet was haphazard and makes interesting telling. During one particular but obscure battle, musketeers, after loosing off all their shot, rammed small knives into the muzzles of their guns and charged the enemy.

In his *Military Antiquities* Grose mentions a regulation of 1686 which sets out details of grenadiers' arms. He says that they were: 'armed with fire-lock, or snap-hance muskets, slings, swords, daggers, and pouches with grenades; they also had hatchets, with which, after firing and throwing their grenades, they were on the word of command 'fell on', to rush upon the enemy. The practise of screwing the dagger into the muzzle of the piece, is also there directed'.

France seems to have set the fashion for a socket fixing. During one of the campaigns of King William III, an engagement took place in Flanders in which three French regiments fixed bayonets by the socket method, a contrivance then unknown in the British army. One of these regiments advanced against the 25th Regiment of Foot with fixed bayonets. Lieut-Col. Maxwell, who commanded the 25th, ordered his men to screw their bayonets into the muzzles of their guns, thinking they meant to decide the affair at close quarters. To his great surprise, when they came within range, the French began to open fire. For a moment his men faltered, not conceiv-

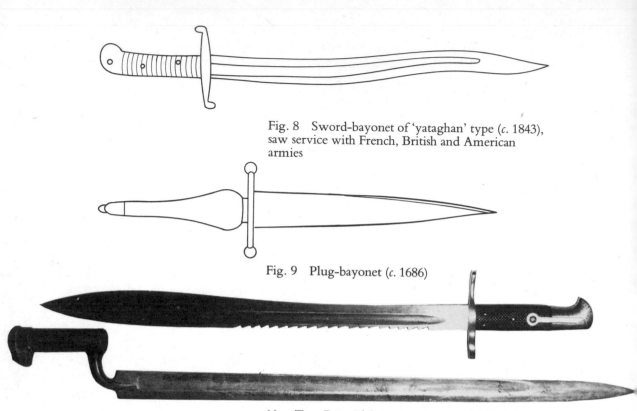

Fig. 8   Sword-bayonet of 'yataghan' type (*c.* 1843), saw service with French, British and American armies

Fig. 9   Plug-bayonet (*c.* 1686)

44.   *Top:* Rare Elcho sword bayonet of 1870. Issued for service in the Ashanti War of 1873–74. *Bottom:* Scarce socket bayonet known as the '1843 Sappers and Miners'. This example differs somewhat from all recorded patterns and could be of foreign derivation, or one made in limited numbers for the Militia

ing it possible to fire with fixed bayonets.

The socket-bayonet was used by the armies of the world until the 1890s, but in Russia was to see service until 1917. The price of bayonets is still reasonable with the exception being the following rare models and patterns: Jacobs; Lancaster ovalbore; Baker; Martini-Henry 'Elcho' and the Australian machette bayonet of 1943. Add to these the almost unobtainable *genuine* plug-bayonet (beware the 'doctored' kitchen knife), and the equally rare kukri-socket bayonet and you have some idea of the valuable specimens which could come your way.

Daggers or fighting knives have always played an important part in the equipment of the soldier but have never really been officially recognised. The British Navy had a small dirk which was more decorative than functional, while the Scottish regiments carried a more lethal dagger hung at the waist or a much smaller version stuck down a stocking top. One of the rarer types of seventeenth century dagger is that known as the 'gunner's stiletto', usually distinguishable by a series of numbers and lines stamped onto the blade. This multi-purpose dagger could be quickly inserted into the bore of a cannon and a correct reading of shot and weight could be ascertained.

In America the 'Bowie knife' and short fighting dagger have always played a major role in close-quarter skirmishes. In both world wars, the trench knife was part of Allied combatants' equipment, with the Americans favouring a leather grip, while their British counterparts plumped for a heavy brass or bronze grip and a murderous stiletto blade. This latter weapon was manufactured by the firm of Wilkinson, and was issued to commando, airborne and other troops likely to find themselves behind enemy lines.

Once the nucleus of a collection has been formed, it is time to start thinking of cleaning and display. For weapons with a heavy coating of rust, a good soaking in a mixture of diesel and paraffin oil is a wise first move. Find an old metal tray long and deep enough to accommodate the whole length (for swords and long bayonets, the ideal thing is one of those long galvanised troughs used to feed free-range chickens), make sure that the sword, dagger or bayonet is completely submerged in the mixture and then leave it for about two weeks. From time to time clean it gently using wire-wool, fine, wet-and-dry emery cloth or, for more stubborn rust, a wire brush. Extreme care should be taken if there are traces of gilt or blueing showing through the dirt. Many fine presentation blades have been completely ruined by over-enthusiastic use of a power drill.

When all the metal parts are as clean as you want them to be, apply a liberal dressing of machine or cycle oil, removing all the surplus with a piece of clean flannel. Brass-work can be tackled with a wadding metal polish or, in the case of extreme verdigris, with a mixture of salt and lemon. Rub gently with the aid of an old toothbrush, wash the mixture off, neutralise it with warm, soapy water, dry the weapon and then finish it with metal polish.

Scabbards and sheaths which were originally blued but bear slight traces of rust should also be gently cleaned, using a pad of fine wire-wool. Leather can be treated with saddle soap or neats-foot oil then finished off with a coating of leather polish.

A good method of display is to mount the collection on peg-board. Find a sturdy wall that is not likely to collapse under the added weight. Batten wall with laths, then screw or nail up the sheets of peg-board. Special hooks can be purchased to give an extra, museum-like touch to the whole setting.

A number of collectors prefer to exhibit their choicest items without scabbard or sheath, but, if you do settle for this method, remember to label or number all those discarded scabbards. Nothing is more annoying than discovering, years later when you decide to exchange or sell a particular piece, that you've misplaced or lost the sheath.

7 Paintings and Prints, Maps, Books and Photographs

Weapons, badges, medals and insignia look very impressive on wall or cabinet but there is little point in collecting them if documentary evidence is lacking. No other field of militaria more graphically reveals the drama, glory and horror of the action that it commemorates. Descriptions of weapons, uniforms, victors and vanquished, all have been faithfully recorded over the years and preserved for posterity. The field is vast and almost endless. It ranges from oil paintings, engravings and pen and ink sketches to silk cigarette cards, postcards, books, documents, scrapbooks, photographs and even posters and stamps.

Although very colourful and full of high-spirited action, many paintings and prints are only artists' impressions and are therefore 'artistically licensed' in their treatment of weapons and equipment. This is not a modern failing only. Biagio di Antonio's *Siege of Troy* shows archers, pikemen and cavalry all bearing arms and equipment of the sixteenth century. Others imagined, without any first-hand experience, the type of weapons carried during a particular battle with some curious results; muskets or pistols with strange-looking locks; cock and hammers that would never fire. Some artists, acknowledging their lack of technical and military knowledge, left out firing mechanisms altogether, giving their subjects a kind of dummy weapon to carry. At the other end of the scale, we have evidence of artists who knew their warfare backwards. One such example is the engraving by Thomas Rowlandson of a unit of 'Sadler's Flying Artillery'. Equipped with light carriages and small swivel guns, they are accompanied by a detachment of cavalry shown discharging flintlock holster pistols at a fleeing enemy. The detail of loading and firing drill is dramatically accurate, even down to the practice of firing a pistol held forward and on one side. With all the vagaries including wind and rain which could afflict him, the galloping trooper stood a better chance of discharging his piece if the priming powder took fire first time. With the pistol held on its side, the chances of losing priming powder were somewhat reduced.

Another painting by W. von Kobell of Bavarian artillery at the siege of Breslau in 1806 shows great detail of arms and equipment – an invaluable aid to military miniature and arms collectors alike.

45.   Engraving of Carabineers *c.* 1590–1640, illustrating various items of their equipment and depicting standard manoeuvres

As a great number of these works are housed in the world's finest galleries and museums, the chances of actually purchasing an original is very remote indeed. However, a few overlooked or unknown examples do find their way onto the market from time to time, so a diligent search through jumble is not entirely a waste of time. Care should be exercised here, however; a few dealers camouflage modern prints and paintings and pass them off as 'antique' originals. This magic transformation is brought about in a number of ways. Their favourite is to add a little 'foxing', a brown staining that is sometimes found on old prints and documents. Paintings are skilfully aged with a mixture of old varnish, stain and the contents of a vacuum cleaner.

Not all fakes are offered to the public through established antique shops, since they run the risk of prosecution for a false description of the offered article. A great number of doctored pieces find their way into suburban auction rooms where they are snapped up by novice traders or inexperienced collectors. If a dealer buys a pup, as everyone has, he either writes it off as a bad buy or, if he cannot afford the loss, pushes it back into another auction. The amateur art collector will most probably rush off home with his purchase and hang it up for all to see. Unless enlightened, the poor chump will cherish it for years and regale one and all with its artistic and financial worth.

Although such faking is rather difficult to detect without proper equipment, it is possible for the novice to ascertain by close inspection if the print or painting has been tampered with. Sometimes a skilful faker will use original materials, but even so there are almost always tell-tale signs of some sort. Pincer marks on pins or nails holding the backing in place are one indication of forgery. If these have been removed or replaced, then there should be a good reason. Was this done to replace the frame or repair damage to the actual picture? In any case, check and double check for it will save you money in the long run.

If you cannot afford or find an original work, the good reproductions which come onto the market from time to time make acceptable alternatives. More interesting items and artists include those listed on page 107.

46.   Black and white reproduction of large (6ft × 4ft) oil painting looted from the Reich Chancellery in Berlin in 1945, and until recently left to lie forgotten in a dusty attic. It commemorates the ceremony of the foundation of the Third Reich in the Garrison Church, Potsdam, and shows Chancellor Adolf Hitler reading his opening speech in the presence of President Hindenburg. Seated just behind and to the left of Hindenburg is Herman Goering

47. Small early nineteenth century oil painting purchased very cheaply by the author after being found on the back of a dust-cart!

Bayeux Tapestry Battle of Hastings 1066. One of the oldest known sources showing good details of chain mail and arms.

Hans Burgkmais Maximilian I, Archduke of Austria and Germanic Emperor (1459–1519) inspecting a cannon foundry.

Martin Martini Battle of Morat, Switzerland, 22 June, 1476. The Swiss routing troops of Burgundy's Charles the Bold.

Hans Holbein the Younger Famous for portraying Swiss fighting forces of that period (1497–1543), with fine detail of arms and armour.

Hans Von Gessdorf A leading Rhenish doctor who wrote an important surgical book *Feldbuch der Wundarznei* (*The Art of Healing Wounds*). Illustrated with twenty-three wood engravings it shows, among other gory details, the extraction of arrow heads and amputation of shattered limbs. The prints are reproduced separately from the book.

Sebastian Vrancx A former captain of the Antwerp Bourgeois Guard who specialised in cavalry skirmishes, he later chose the ravages and atrocities of the Thirty Years' War as subject matter for his many colourful paintings.

Franz Josef Beich (1662–1726) Commissioned by Maximilian II Emmanuel to paint the siege of Neuhäusel.

Philips Wouwerman Seventeenth-century painter who captured in his works all the vicious fury of cavalry and pikemen at war.

Joseph Vernet One of his finest works was a painting of an artillery park at Toulon. Executed during the eighteenth century, it portrays banks of cannon, cannon-balls and even gunsmiths at work.

During the American War of Independence, many artists took up pen and brush to capture highlights of this revolutionary struggle. Most famous of all these works must be Paul Revere's *The Son of Liberty*. This pictures the Boston Massacre of 5 March, 1770, in which a section of the 29th British Regiment fired into a crowd of marchers in King Street, killing five. John Trumbull, who was present at the Battle of Bunker Hill (17 June, 1775), captured in his painting the ranks of stalwart hunters and farmers holding off the cream of the British infantry.

A wide selection of both prints and paintings of the Napoleonic Wars still exists. Such artists as L. F. Lejeune, Naudet, Horace Vernet, Adolphe Roehn, Bacler d'Albe, W. von Kobell, A. Kirchenko, Peter Hess and Lady Butler all contribute greatly to a fine and stirring battle panorama. And so the list and the years roll on – to the China Wars, Crimean War, American Civil War, South African Wars, all contributing information for the student of military history. Weapons, uniforms, insignia, even modes of transportation have changed over the years and all are preserved in painting or print.

48. Memento of the Boer War in South Africa, 1899–1902. Head-scarf bearing the words and music of a popular ditty of the day – *The Absent-minded Beggar* by Rudyard Kipling, with music by Arthur Sullivan.

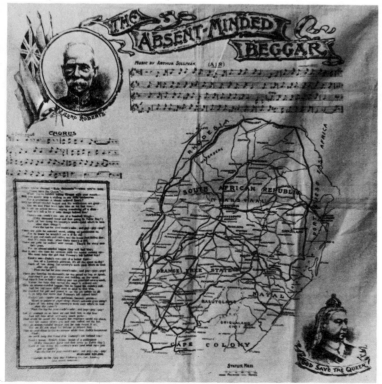

Maps, Books and Photographs

Maps too, hold a certain fascination for some collectors setting out as they do the details of regimental strongholds either just prior to, or immediately after a battle. Searching long and diligently through piles of secondhand books, one can often find such items folded away between the pages. Some are already coloured or tinted but for those of you with an artistic flair many long winter evenings will quickly pass if you colour your own.

Books, like prints and paintings, tell much and many contemporary accounts help us understand the evolution of militaria. For example, the red tunics so bright and gay served a double purpose. Not only could staff officers see for themselves just where their men were but the red material also concealed the presence of bullet wounds and ensuing gore. Nothing demoralised a good soldier more quickly than seeing a companion spouting blood.

Here are a few books which will enhance any collection.

Exercise of Firelock, no author (London, 1712)
Our Engines of War, H. J. Jervis (London, 1859)
Military Antiquities Respecting A History of the English Army, 2 Vols, F. Grose, (1812)
Naval and Military Costumes, J. Atkinson (London, 1807)
Biographia Navalis, J. Charnock (London, 1794)
Naval Biographical Dictionary, W. O'Byrne (London, 1849)
Exercise for Broadsword, B. Wayne (Washington, 1850)
Dress of the British Soldier, J. Luard (London, 1852)
Cavalry, L. Nolan (London, 1853)
Ranks and Badges, O. L. Perry (London, 1887)
Old Scottish Regimental Colours, A. Ross (Edinburgh, 1885)
Chats on Military Curios, A. C. Johnson, (London, 1915)
Cromwell's Army, C. H. Firth (London, 1902)
Famous Regiments of the British Army, W. H. Davenport Adams (London, 1864)
Textbook for Officers at School of Musketry (London, 1877)
Remarks on Rifle Guns, E. Baker (London, 1835)
Inventory and Survey of the Armouries of the Tower of London, 2 Vols, C. J. Ffoulkes (London, 1916)
Sword, Lance and Bayonet – A record of the Arms of the British Army and Navy, C. J. Ffoulkes and E. C. Hopkinson (Cambridge, 1938)
The Rifleman's Manual, H. Busk (London, 1890)
Deane's Manual of the History and Science of Firearms (London, 1858)
A Treatise on Naval Gunnery, Sir H. Douglas (London, 1855)
The Artillerist's Manual, F. A. Griffiths (1859)

49.   *Above:* Engraving from *Bernard's British History. c.* 1785, showing 'A real representation of the dress of An American Rifle-man'.

50.   *Right:* A regimental beer stein originally belonging to a bombardier in 3rd Prussian Guard Field Artillery. The owner's name and details of two years' service are incorporated in the design

Loading at Breech and Loading at Muzzle for Military Weapons, etc., Westly Richards (London, 1863)

Fixed Bayonets, A. Hutton (London, 1890)

Suggestions for the Cleaning and Management of Percussion Arms, G. Lovell (1842)

Wellington's Army 1809–1814, C. W. C. Oman (London, 1913)

The Crossbow, Medieval and Modern, Sir R. Payne-Gallway (London, 1903)

Ancient Armour and Weapons in Europe, 3 Vols, J. Hewitt (London, 1855)

Abridgements of Patent Specifications Relating to Firearms and Other Weapons, Ammunition and Accoutrements, 1588–1858, H. M. Patent Office (London, 1859)

The Scottish Highlands, Highland Clans and Highland Regiments, John Wilson (Edinburgh and London)
Arms and Armour at Sandringham, C. Clarke (London, 1910)
Japanese Armour from the Inside, Matthew Garbutt (London, 1914)

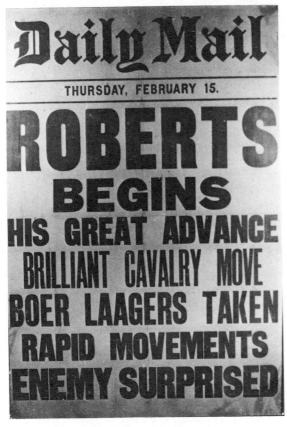

51. A fascinating and unusual piece of militaria – a well-preserved *Daily Mail* poster announcing Lord Roberts' great advance in South Africa which eventually brought victory over the stubbornly resisting Boers

Chinese Weapons, E. T. C. Werner, Royal Asiatic Society (Shanghai, 1932)
A Glossary of the Construction, Decoration and Use of Arms and Armour in all Countries and in all Times, together with some closely related subjects, George Cameron Stone (Portland, Maine, 1934)
Ancient Scottish Weapons, J. Drummond and J. Anderson (London)
A record of European Armour and Arms through Seven Centuries, 5 Vols, (London, 1920–2)
The ABC of War Medals and Decorations, W. Augustus Steward (London, 1918)

Other items well worth a particular search are the pay-books and discharge parchments of pre-1881 soldiers who, if unable to sign their names, made a mark instead,

52. Selection of German, French and British postcards with military connections

53. Cleverly executed fake gun-case labels. The top two purport to be of the famous gunsmith H. W. Mortimer, the lower of a well-known Irish gunsmith, W. E. Rigby. All had been 'aged' almost overnight in a mixture of coffee and boot polish!

an illuminating reminder that the last century was, in many respects, another age. Medal rolls, closely linked with medals, also make for an interesting collection. A man's whole army career is mapped out from start to finish on these odd bits of paper. Many end up in the dustbin or waste-paper bin once an old warrior has passed to his final rest. A talk with your local refuse collector or scrap merchant could pay dividends.

Indeed, I can vouch that even casual conversations can throw light on unsolved puzzles. An American friend, forming a collection of Crimea medals, managed to purchase a roll to go with one of his pieces. On the roll under 'Remarks', he came across 'H. & R.' repeated six times on one sheet. Nobody could guess what this meant, and it was only when a client of mine, knowing my interest in this particular problem, went out of his way to search through some of the old medal lists that the

54.   For collectors of military music, *It's a Long Way to Tipperary* printed on a head-scarf during World War I

puzzle was solved. After some while he found what he was looking for: Hunt & Roskill, Medallist and Silversmith. Their name can be sometimes found on the ornate medal clasps which officers had made to suspend their Crimea or Baltic medals from.

Post cards and cigarette cards are another worthwhile avenue of research. Badges, flags, helmets and uniforms of most of the world's leading military powers during the late nineteenth and early twentieth century have been depicted on them. They can be purchased either in albums or in loose lots. Collectors are advised to specialise in complete sets but, if the subject is unusual, even one or two cards are better than nothing at all.

An increasingly popular item for collection is the gun-case label. With antique gun and pistol cases now fetching such huge prices (not to mention the actual price of the weapon itself), collectors have taken to sticking in their collections an example of some of the better known gunsmith's labels, carrying such names as H. W. Mortimer and William Rigby. These labels, up to the turn of the century were collected by gentlefolk and preserved in scrapbooks, together with valentine and birthday cards. As with other branches of militaria, fakes are coming onto the market and those illustrated hail from the USA. These have been reproduced by a photographic process then stained and treated in a mixture of coffee and boot polish. The best way to detect these is to take a good sniff at them.

The American Civil War period has produced numerous interesting photographs. These are now greatly sought after by collector and dealer for, just like the early paintings and prints, they hold a wealth of detail and information.

Soldiers throughout the ages have always been renowned for their looting habits and the two world wars were no exception. Apart from the usual bric-à-brac of watches, cameras and household ware, some lads took it into their heads to take photographs. Lifted from deserted houses or dead bodies, they covered all sorts of subjects. Aircraft, tanks, ships and wrecked landing craft, now long forgotten and destroyed, are preserved on the small shiny squares of photographic paper. For the experienced collector and researcher they reveal much. Numbers on aircraft, tanks and even lorries can be traced, building up a picture of just what regiment or flight they were originally attached to. With German and Italian subjects, one is able to establish the identity of various pieces of uniform or equipment that were utilised from time to time. Although regulations *may* have stipulated that such and such an item would only be worn or used during a certain period, our photographic evidence tells us otherwise.

When storing documents, maps or parchments, it is advisable to choose a place which is well ventilated and free from damp. If you can afford it, then a largeish architect's plan chest capable of holding items up to Double Elephant size ($42\frac{1}{4} \times 30\frac{1}{2}$ inches – inside drawer size) will certainly solve the storage problem. Failing this, a good substitute would be a large chest of drawers. It is most important to keep the collection flat so as to avoid creasing. Extensive fold marks can be removed or, at the least, improved by pressing with a warm flat-iron. Care should be exercised however, for brandishing an iron that is too warm will result in a scorched and brittle antique document, likely to disintegrate at the first touch. Parchment should not be ironed and on no account should it be allowed to become damp, for this will encourage mildew.

Cleaning stained or foxed documents calls for a delicate touch. It is possible to carry this out yourself, but a close study of the process should precede the operation. Practise on a few worthless or unimportant prints for a while just to get the general hang of the business. In any case, I recommend a handbook entitled *Maps and Prints for Profit and Pleasure* by D. Gohm, for all keen collectors.

8 War Medals

Since the dawn of time, men, however savage, have bestowed various awards upon one another for acts of bravery in battle. To this day we find tribes in Central Africa and the Amazon following customs initiated centuries ago; shrunken heads, scalp-locks and testicles are nothing more than a form of war medal, a mark of esteem and a badge to exhibit, testifying to the honourable acquittal of the wearer in action.

Medals as such can be traced back to the Ancient Egyptians and Romans, where plaques of brass and copper were awarded for outstanding feats of bravery. As these awards were sometimes too cumbersome and weighty for personal adornment, they ended up as part and parcel of horse equipment, the origin of the ever-popular horse brass. During the Middle Ages, a warrior, knighted on the field of battle, was permitted to carry a square, instead of a swallow-tailed, pennant and also to use a war cry, from which we trace the origin of the coat of arms.

The variety and number of awards seemed to fluctuate with different monarchs. The rank and file were usually rewarded with money. A Sergeant Weems of the 1st Royals, who, during the battle of Sedgemoor (6 July, 1685), served the great guns with verve and tenacity was given a gratuity of £40. Among the first medals to be officially recognised and classed as such are those awarded by Elizabeth I after the great defeat of the Spanish Armada in 1588 – but these were awarded, as was the practice then, only to leading officers. These were struck in gold and silver, having rings and chains for hanging, probably from the neck. During the troubled reign of James I, we have a medal almost identical to the Elizabethan one, known in collecting circles as the 'Ark-in-Flood' medal. There are two kinds of obverse to this medal, one has the portrait bust of the King in armour with a ruff, and the legend 'FIDEI DEFENSOR' encircling the head. This apparently was for military officers and the other, bearing an obverse with the King's head surmounted by a broad-brimmed hat, for his courtiers, although there is dispute on this point. The motto on the obverse of the second type reads 'JACOBUS · D · G · MAG · BRITA · FR · ET · HI · REX' and on the reverse is an ark within an oval band containing the motto 'PER VNDUS SEVAS TRANQVILLA'.

Medals for actual military prowess were established at the instigation of Charles I.

They were, according to the order of a Court, held at Oxford on 18 May, 1643, 'to be delivered to wear on the breast of every man who shall be certified under the hands of their commander-in-chief to have done us faithful service in the forlorn hope'. These medals were only, as can be seen, awarded for very distinguished conduct in the field. Rather rare, one bore the Royal image on the obverse and Prince Charles on the reverse; the other the bust of Charles on the obverse with the inscription 'CAROLUS · D · G · MAG · BRI · FR · ET · HIB · REX', and on the reverse the Royal Arms with the Garter bearing the motto 'HONI · SOIT · QUI · MAL · Y · PENSE'. These two oval medals were struck in silver and are 1·7in×1·3in, and 1·5in×1·2in.

It was at the first battle of the Civil War, Edgehill, on 23 October, 1642, that we have the first recorded award for conspicuous conduct in the field. It was made to an Irish Commander when he recovered a Royal Standard and various items of important military equipment. The soldier in question, Sir Robert Welch as he was to become, was presented with an oval gold medal specially cut to the King's specification by the Royal 'graver of seals and medals', Thomas Rawlins. This medal, ordered by the King on 1 June, 1643, bore on the obverse his own figure and that of his son Prince Charles, and on the reverse a facsimile of the banner Welch saved at Edgehill. The medal, oval in form, was 1·7in×1·5in.

Oliver Cromwell, the puritanical bigot dubbed 'Lord of the Fens', was, by and large, instrumental in forming an army with a 'new look'. One good product of Cromwell's reign was the introduction of the first campaign medal which was awarded to officers and men alike. Although not strictly a medal as we know it – this one being suspended by a chain from the neck – it was to be one of the first medals awarded to all ranks. Known as the Dunbar medal, it was struck on 3 September, 1650, to commemorate the defeat of the Scots Royalists at Dunbar. Designed by the medallist Thomas Simon, it was struck in two sizes: a gold specimen, measuring 1in × 0·85in, for officers; and a silver example, 1·35in × 1·15in for other ranks. On the obverse of this medal we find the bust of Cromwell in armour with the inscription in a semi-circle above, 'WORD AT DVNBAR THE LORD OF HOSTS SEPTEM Y3 · 1650'. The reverse shows an interior view of the House of Commons. Bronze medals do exist but the reverses of these are plain.

With Charles II back on the throne, there is no record of any more military medals being struck. Similarly, there is no record during the reign of James II, William and Mary or Queen Anne, although naval medals of a sort were issued to commemorate victories over the Dutch, while in Anne's reign (1702–14), a large silver medal was struck, apparently for the Navy. The reign of George I reveals nothing in the shape of a medal, while in that of George II there appear to be only a couple – one for the battle of Culloden (16 April 1746), where the Duke of Cumberland so deservedly earned his nickname of 'The Butcher', and the other for taking Louisbourg in Canada on 27 July 1758, where after a seven-week siege, the French garrison was forced to surrender to General Amherst.

It was to be the Honourable East India Company who set the vogue by awarding a medal to their native officers in 1766, when they quelled a mutiny among European troops at Morighyr, and again in 1778 and 1792 when they helped to overthrow Hyder Ali and his son Tippoo Sahib. Although not official or Sovereign awards, they are very much in demand in collecting circles and command a very high price when offered on the open market.

During this period it became customary for certain high-ranking British naval officers to have medals struck privately as awards for their own men. Usually copies of the official awards they had been awarded, the medals were struck in bronze, pewter, tin or lead. As the thought of loot was the driving force behind any battle in that day and age, the value of the spoils determined the material of the medal the recipients could expect to receive.

It was not until after the battle of Waterloo, when Great Britain and her allies finally brought about the downfall of the French and Napoleon, that the first official war medal, the 1815 Waterloo medal, was struck. Students of military history may rush to say that the Naval General Service and Military General Service medals (NGS and MGS), awarded to participants in the many wars from 1793–1840 (NGS) and 1793–1814 (MGS), should take priority but these were not, in fact, awarded until 1848. Struck in silver, the Waterloo medal bore the head of the Prince Regent on the obverse while the reverse carried the winged figure of Victory seated on a plinth with 'WATERLOO, June 18th 1815' beneath, and the name 'WELLINGTON' above. This award was suggested by the Duke of Wellington, and his name is always associated with the introduction of British war medals. An outstanding feature of this first war medal is the instructions issued when awarding it, that 'the ribbon issued with the medal shall never be worn but with the medal suspended to it'.

From this period onward, we find medals struck for nearly every engagement. Some countries, like Germany and Russia, followed Great Britain almost at once, while others used former Orders and decorations struck for nobility and downgraded them. So, from a period of no medals at all, we come through the many wars that helped to forge the Empire, through two world wars, Korea, Malaya and Aden, the minor skirmishes in Suez, Hong Kong, and the bloodbath of Northern Ireland, most of these with their own award.

Enthusiasm in collecting anything is something that every budding collector must possess for without it they will surely burn themselves out within the first few exciting months. However, there is a fine dividing line between keenness and outright fanaticism, for if you tend to live and breathe from dawn to dusk thinking of nothing else but your collection you can soon lapse over that line. Make collecting

55. *Left:* The Waterloo medal awarded to Robert Offer, 3rd Battalion, Grenadier Guards, with original riband and ring suspension.   56. *Right:* Reverse of Waterloo medal, this time awarded to Samuel Smith, also of 3rd Battalion, Grenadier Guards, who was wounded in the battle. The silver suspension is comparatively modern

a pleasure and you will find it a most rewarding hobby.

Discrimination, once again, should be the keynote of your collection. Decide from the beginning just what you want to collect; Army, Navy, Stars, Long Service or Good Conduct medals, perhaps even a range of medals of Queen Victoria's long reign, all make an interesting study. Don't try to collect everything. In this way you will only skim the surface and miss many worthwhile and unusual special pieces.

Like almost all other collectors' items, the history of these medals is often as absorbing as the finding of them.

WATERLOO MEDAL 1815

This was the first British official war medal and can be found with either the official steel ring or unofficial bar suspender. Some collectors jibe at the latter method of suspension, thinking that it detracts from the medal's value. This is of course a matter of opinion, the original large (1in) steel ring run through a steel clip was not always secure, and, as a result, the possessors of this medal frequently had a more ornate silver suspender made according to their wealth or taste. The ribbon is 1½in (sometimes 2in wide), dark crimson with blue edges.

Every schoolboy knows the history of the battle of Waterloo, so I shall not bore the reader with a mundane account. Instead, we will try to catch a glimpse of the action in which some 3,825 British soldiers perished. The French numbered 90,000 and the allied forces 74,400. An overture by an artillery orchestra more than 200 strong opened the day.

The loss in individual regiments was terrible. Four hundred men of the 27th were mowed down in a square without firing a single shot. (Their medals in extra-fine condition are very rare and so extremely expensive.) The 92nd, reduced to some 200 men, made a daring attack upon a column of 2,000 French, and, with the aid of the Scots Greys, routed them. Time and time again the best of the French army assisted by a murderous artillery bombardment drove deep into the squared ranks of the British. The King's Own German Legion was completely routed by the French, while seventy-seven squadrons made a desperate effort to pierce those stubborn but swiftly thinning lines of British infantry.

In vain did the ten battalions of the French Imperial Guard, led by Marshal Ney, push their way up the slopes between Hougomont and La Haye Sainte. The Foot Guards, with the 52nd, 71st and 92nd Regiments, offered such a murderous reception that the French Guards turned and fled in disorder.

The following regiments were present at Waterloo: 2 squadrons, 1st and 2nd Life Guards; 2 squadrons, Royal Horse Guards (Blues); 1st Dragoon Guards; 1st Royals*; 2nd Royal North British Dragoons (Scots Greys)*; 6th Inniskilling Dragoons*; 12th, 13th, 16th Queen's and 23rd Light Dragoons; 7th, 10th Royal; 15th King's; 18th Hussars; 2nd and 3rd Battalions, 1st Foot Guards (Grenadiers); 2nd Battalion, 2nd Foot Guards (Coldstreams); 3rd Battalion, 3rd Foot Guards (Scots Guards); 3rd Battalion, 1st Royal Scots; 1st Battalion, 4th; 3rd Battalion, 14th; 1st Battalion, 23rd Royal Welsh Fusiliers; 1st Battalion, 27th Inniskilling*; 1st Battalion, 28th (Gloucesters); 2nd Battalion, 30th; 1st Battalion, 32nd; 33rd; 1st Battalion, 40th; 1st Battalion, 42nd (Black Watch)*; 2nd Battalion, 44th; 51st; 1st Battalion, 52nd; 2nd Battalion, 69th; 1st Battalion, 71st (Highland Light Infantry); 2nd Battalion, 73rd Perthshires; 1st Battalion, 79th (Cameron Highlanders); 1st Battalion, 92nd (Gordon Highlanders); 1st, 2nd, and Prov. Battalions, 95th; 8 Troops, Royal Horse Artillery; 6 Brigades, Royal Artillery; Corps of Royal Artillery Drivers; Royal Foot Artillery; Royal Engineers; Royal Sappers and Miners; Royal Waggon Train; Field Train Department of the Ordnance; Royal Staff Corps; Commissariat Dept; Ordnance Medical Department. Also present were the following units of the King's German Legion: 1st and 2nd Light Dragoons; 1st, 2nd, and 3rd Hussars; 1st, 2nd, 3rd, 4th, 5th, and 8th Line Battalions, and 1st and 2nd Light Battalions, the total present being about 2,308 officers and 42,120 non-commissioned officers and men. (Medals marked '*' are very rare and always command a high price.)

NAVAL GENERAL SERVICE MEDAL 1793–1840

As we have already mentioned this medal was awarded to men serving from 1793, but was not issued until 1848. The obverse bears the head of young Queen Victoria and the date '1848'. The reverse shows a seated figure of Britannia upon the back of a sea-horse, with a laurel branch in her left hand and a trident in her right. The suspension clasp is plain and in silver as is the medal. The ribbon is a wide section of white, edged with navy blue.

Men who could lay claim to this medal served with the 'Wooden Walls of Old England' and in the struggle against many of England's enemies saw service against the French at Trafalgar and the Nile under Lord Nelson. Even a baby won a NGS – one 'Baby' Daniel Tremendous McKenzie who was born just before the battle of 1 June 1794 aboard HMS *Tremendous*. This may seem curious but it was the custom to allow certain seamen to take their wives to sea with them. Apart from cooking, sewing and other general chores, it is recorded that these women helped serve the great guns when called upon to do so. One women was known to have claimed, and actually received this medal after doing battle at Trafalgar on 21 October 1805. However, Jane Townshend who served aboard HMS *Defiance* hadn't reckoned with the Lords of the Admiralty; later, this award was rescinded and struck off the Rolls. There are 230 different engagement bars in all, bearing either the name of the ship involved, the name of the action, or the words 'BOAT SERVICE'. In some cases medals will be found named for Army personnel who served aboard His Majesty's ships instead of the usual contingent of Royal Marines. Accepted claims for the NGS totalled 20,900.

It was around this time that Matthew Boulton, the partner of James Watt of the famous Soho Works near Birmingham, decided to strike medals and present one to each participant in the fight. The medal bears on the obverse a fine bust of Nelson, with an inscription surrounding it: 'HORATIO VISCOUNT NELSON. K.B. DUKE OF BRONTE'. On the reverse the battle is represented *en cameo*, with the famous signal, 'England expects every man to do his duty', on the ribbon running round the outside of the medal, and, in the exergue, 'TRAFALGAR OCT. 21 1805'. On the edge of the medal is the inscription: 'TO THE HEROES OF TRAFALGAR FROM M. BOULTON'. Struck in silver for senior officers and pewter for junior officers and men, they did not appeal to the latter, who either refused them outright or threw them overboard. Those who did retain them wore them suspended from a blue ribbon. A few proof copies were struck in bronze.

Yet another award, thought to have been struck at the instance of Nelson's agent, Mr Alexander Davison, was presented to every officer and seaman of Nelson's fleet: gold to captains and lieutenants; silver to warrant officers; bronze-gilt to petty officers and bronze to seamen and marines. Upon the edge is impressed 'FROM ALEXANDER DAVISON ESQ., ST. JAMES SQUARE: A TRIBUTE OF

REGARD'. This medal, modelled by C. H. Küchler and $1\frac{7}{8}$ in in diameter, was issued unnamed, but many recipients had their names together with the name of their ship engraved above the skyline on the reverse. Although they were worn suspended from a broad blue ribbon, they were not officially sanctioned.

On the obverse there is a standing figure of Britannia holding aloft in her right hand a branch, while tucked under her left arm is a rather outsize shield bearing the profile of Nelson. The wording, 'REAR ADMIRAL LORD NELSON OF THE NILE', stretches around the outer surface. The reverse depicts nearly thirty ships manoeuvring into battle positions, with the sun on the horizon spreading its rays to the sky. In the exergue is 'VICTORY OF THE NILE AUGUST 1. 1798', and, above the battle scene on the ribbon, 'ALMIGHTY GOD HAS BLESSED HIS MAJESTY'S ARMS'.

Bars with the names of the action thereon Although many bars were issued with the NGS medal, six is the most awarded to any one man. There exists one example which boasts five bars. Awarded to Thos. Hewitt, midshipman, for '1 JUNE 1794', '12 OCTR 1798', '4 FEB BOAT SERVICE 1804', 'CENTAUR 26 AUGT 1800', and 'ALGIERS'. Another, awarded to Captain (later Rear-Admiral Sir Thomas) Ussher, Kt., C.B., K.C.H., has '1 JUNE 1794', 'REDWING 7 MAY 1808', 'REDWING 31ST MAY 1808', 'MAGALA 29TH APRIL 1812', and '2 MAY BOAT SERVICE 1813'. This is a particularly rare set of bars, for only seven of the second were issued, five of the third, seven of the fourth, and forty-nine of the fifth.

NYMPH, 18 June 1793. 4 issued. Capture of the French frigate *Cleopatra*. Captain E. Pellew, who commanded the *Nymph*, was knighted.

CRESCENT, 20 Oct. 1793. Capture of the French frigate *Reunion*, which was seconded to the Royal Navy under the same name.

ZEBRA, 7 March 1794. 2 issued. Running the *Zebra* sloop alongside the bastion of Fort Royal at Martinique, and storming and capturing the fort.

CARYSFORT, 29 May 1794. None issued. Recapture of the *Caster*.

1 JUNE 1794 ('The Glorious First of June'). 576 issued. Defeat of the French fleet by Lord Howe, capture of 6 sail of the line and 1 sunk. Principal vessels engaged were H.M. ships *Queen Charlotte, Royal Sovereign, Royal George, Barfleur, Bellerophon, Impregnable, Queen, Caesar, Culloden, Defence, Glory, Gibraltar, Invincible, Majestic, Leviathan, Marlborough, Montague, Ramillies, Russell, Orion, Thunderer, Tremendous, Audacious, Alfred, Brunswick, Valiant*, the frigates, *Aquilon, Latona, Phaeton, Niger, Southampton, Venus, Charon, Pegasus*, the sloops, *Comet, Incendiary*, and the cutters, *Ranger* and *Rattler*.

ROMENY, 17 June 1794. 2 issued. Capture of French frigate *Sybille*.

BLANCHE, 4 Jan. 1795. 5 issued. At the end of the battle her crew numbered but 190 men. Capture of the French frigate *Pique*.

LIVELY, 13 March 1795. 3 issued. Capture of the French frigate *Tourterelle*.

14 MARCH 1795, 111 issued. Action with French fleet and capture of 2 sail of line. 22 vessels under Vice-Admiral Hotham were engaged.

ASTRAEA, 10 April 1795. 2 issued. Capture of the French frigate *Gloire*.

THETIS, 17 May 1795 (3 issued) and HUSSAR, 17 May 1795 (1 issued). Action with four French ships, and capture of *La Raison* and *Prevoyante*.

MOSQUITO, 9 June 1795. None issued. Brought about by the loss of captain and crew soon after the engagement.

17 JUNE 1795. 38 issued. Seven vessels engaged with a brilliant repulse by Vice-Admiral Cornwallis, of a fleet four times superior in strength.

23 JUNE 1795. 201 issued. Action under Admiral Lord Bridport with French fleet, and the capture of 3 sail of the line; the *Formidable* became the British ship *Belleisle*, and the *Tigre* was also added under its own name. The *Alexander* was a recapture. 29 vessels engaged.

DIDO, 23 June 1795 (1 issued) and LOWESTOFFE, 23 June 1795 (6 issued). Action with the French frigates *Minerve* and *Artemise*, with capture of the former.

SPIDER, 25 Aug. 1795. 1 only issued. Action with two French brigs.

PORT SPERGUI, 17 March 1796. 4 issued to survivors of the *Diamond*, *Liberty*, and *Aristocrat*. Destroying the batteries at Port Spergui, and destroying the corvette *Etourdie*, 4 brigs, 2 sloops, and 1 lugger.

INDEFATIGABLE, 20 April 1796. 6 issued. Capture of the French frigate *Virginia*, in the English Channel.

UNICORN, 8 June 1796 (4 issued) and SANTA MARGARITA, 8 June 1796 (3 issued). Action with 3 French frigates *La Tribune*, *La Tamise* and *La Legere*, and capture of the two former.

SOUTHAMPTON, 9 June 1796. 4 issued. Capture of French corvette *Utile*.

DRYAD, 13 June 1796. 7 issued. Capture of the French frigate *Proserpine* which became HMS *Amelia*.

TERPSICHORE, 13 Oct. 1796. 3 issued. Capture of the Spanish frigate *Mahonesa*.

LAPWING, 8 Dec. 1796. 2 issued. Action with French ship *Décieux* and brig *Vaillante*, with the capture of former.

MINERVA, 19 Dec. 1796 (5 issued) and BLANCHE, 19 Dec. 1796 (2 issued). Capture of Spanish frigate *Santa Sabina* by the *Minerva* and action between *Blanche* and *Ceres*.

INDEFATIGABLE, 13 Jan. 1797 (8 issued) and AMAZON, 13 Jan. 1797 (6 issued). Destruction of French *Droits de L'Homme*, off the coast of France. The *Amazon* blown ashore and her crew taken prisoner.

ST. VINCENT, 14 Feb. 1797. 363 issued. Action with the Spanish fleet resulting in the capture of 4 sail of the line. This battle was one of the most stirring events of the period with Commodore Horatio Nelson really stealing the thunder from his senior officers. On St. Valentine's Day, 1797, the battle of St Vincent was fought between the Spanish fleet of 27 ships of the line and 8 frigates under Admiral Don Josef de Cordova, and 20 British ships of the line, 2 sloops and a cutter. The British ships had been cruising off the coasts of Spain and Portugal to prevent the combined fleets of the allies, Spain, Holland and France, from joining forces. Sir John Jervis commanded; his flagship was the *Victory*. Passing through the 2 divisions of the Spanish fleet, he cut off 9 of the enemies' vessels. The Spaniards then attempted to break the British line, but the effort was frustrated, 2 of the enemy's ships striking their colours. This action, which only lasted 4 hours, resulted in the loss of 4 ships by the enemy, Commodore Horatio Nelson of the *Captain*, sporting 74 guns, took the *San Josef* of 112 guns, and the *San Nicolas* of 80 guns.

In this battle Nelson, by his intrepid action, placed himself in the front ranks of commanders, and his bravery and verve were rewarded by the Order of the Bath, and his advancement to the rank of Rear-Admiral. In the fight off St Vincent he not only attacked at close quarters the *Santissima Trinidad*, a great galleon of 112 guns, but, with the aid of the *Culloden* (Captain Trowbridge), which gallantly started the engagement, he fought for nearly an hour this great ship and four other galleons which had come to her assistance. Then the *Blenheim* (Captain Frederick), and the *Excellent* (Captain Collingwood) came to assist the English, and Nelson ran the *Captain* alongside the *San Nicolas*, quickly sprang through one of the stern windows, and, leading his men across the Spaniard's deck, boldly boarded the *San Josef*, on the quarter-deck of which he soon received the swords of the conquered officers.

By five o'clock the Spanish were in retreat, having lost to their enemy 4 of their finest vessels, and, besides receiving a blow to their naval power, had considerably minimised their value to the French in their effort to command the Channel, and upset the calculations of the Dutch. For the victory, Sir John Jervis was created Earl of St Vincent, and awarded a pension of £3,000 per annum, while the unfortunate Spanish Admiral was relieved of his post.

The vessels engaged in this action were: HM ships *Victory, Britannia, Barfleur, Blenheim, Prince George, Captain, Goliath, Excellent, Egmont, Culloden, Colossus, Diadem, Namur, Orion, Irresistible*, the frigates, *Dido, Lively, Minerva, Niger* and *Southampton*, the sloops, *Bon Citoyenne* and *Raven*, and the cutter *Fox*.

SAN FIORENZO, 8 March 1797. 7 issued. Capture of *Resistance* and *Constance*. The first named became the *Fisgard*.

NYMPHE, 8 March 1797. 6 issued.

CAMPERDOWN, 11 Oct. 1797. 332 issued. Battle of Camperdown, when Admiral Duncan defeated the Dutch fleet.

PHOEBE, 21 Dec. 1797. 7 issued. Capture of the French frigate *Nereide*, which was added to the British Navy under the same name.

123

MARS, 21 April 1798. 26 issued. Capture of French 74 gun, *L'Hercule*. In this bitter action the *Mars* lost her captain, Alexander Hood.

ISLE ST MARCOU, 6 May 1798. 3 issued. Action at the Island of Marcou. 2 boats engaged.

LION, 15 July 1798. 21 issued. Action with 4 Spanish frigates and capture of the *Santa Dorotea*, which was added to the British Navy under the same name.

NILE, 1 Aug. 1798. 251 issued Battle of the Nile. Fifteen ships engaged: *Vanguard*, *Bellerophon*, *Orion*, *Culloden*, *Zealous*, *Audacious*, *Defiance*, *Minotaur*, *Goliath*, *Leander*, *Majestic*, *Alexander*, *Swiftsure*, *Theseus*, and the sloop, *Mutine*.

ESPOIR, 7 Aug. 1798. 1 issued. Action with and capture of Genoese pirate ship, *La Guria*.

12 Oct. 1798. 81 issued. Action under Sir J. B. Warren with a French squadron, and capture of the *Hoche* a 74 – which became the *Donegal* – and two frigates. Eight ships engaged.

FISGARD II, 20 Oct. 1799. 9 issued. Capture of the French frigate *l'Immortalite*.

SYBILLE, 28 Feb. 1799. 12 issued. Capture of the French *La Forte* after a stiff fight in which a detachment of the Scotch Brigade, which was aboard the *Sybille*, took part.

TELEGRAPH, 18 March 1799. None issued. Capture of *L'Hirondelle II*.

ACRE, 30 May 1799. 42 issued. This bar is inscribed: 'ACRE 30 MAY 1799'. However, as the French raised the siege on May 20th, with Napoleon retreating and leaving twenty-three of his guns, the bar is wrongly inscribed. It is nevertheless official. This bar was awarded to those who assisted the Turkish fleet to defend *Acre* from the French attack, the ships taking part under Commodore Sir Henry Smith being the *Theseus*, *Tigre* and *Alliance*.

SCHIERMONIKOOG, 12 Aug. 1799. 10 issued.

ARROW, 13 Sept. 1799. 2 issued. Action and capture of *Draak* and *Gier*. Two vessels. The other boat was the *Wolverine*, but no bar was issued for that.

SURPRISE with HERMIONE, 25 Oct. 1799. 7 issued. Boarding and recapture of the *Hermione*. For this outstanding action Captain Hamilton was knighted.

SPEEDY, 6 Nov. 1799. 3 issued. Action with ten Spanish and two schooners, with successful defence of a convoy.

COURIER, 22 Nov. 1799. 3 issued. Action with and capture of the *Guerrier*.

VIPER, 26 Dec. 1799. 2 issued. Capture of the French brig *Furet*.

FAIRY, 5 Feb. 1800 (4 issued) and HARPY, 5 Feb. 1800 (4 issued). Action with and capture of the French frigate *Pallas*, which later became HMS *Pique*.

PETEREL, 21 March 1800. 2 issued. Capture of *La Liguerienne*.

PENELOPE, 30 March 1800 (11 issued) and VINCIEGO, 30 March 1800 (2 issued). Night action with *Guillaume Tell*. The *Lion* and *Foudroyant* were also engaged and they actually captured the vessel, which later became HMS *Malta*, but no award was made to the surviving crews of these ships.

124

DÉSIRÉE, 8 July 1800. 23 issued. Boarding and capturing the French frigate *Désirée*, and other French vessels. Eighteen vessels engaged.

SEINE, 20 Aug. 1800. 9 issued. Capture of French frigate *Vengeance*, between San Domingo and Porto Rico.

PHOEBE, 19 Feb. 1801. 7 issued. Capture of French frigate *Africaine* which later became HMS *Amelia*.

EGYPT. 626 issued. For services on and around the coast of Egypt. One hundred and seventeen vessels were engaged.

COPENHAGEN, 1801. 589 issued. Thirty-eight vessels engaged.

SPEEDY, 6 May. 7 issued. Capture of the *Gamo*.

GUT OF GIBRALTAR, 12 July 1801. 152 issued. Ten ships engaged. Action with the French squadrons in the *Gut of Gibraltar*, and destruction of two Spanish ships of 122 guns each, and the capture of the *St Antonio*, a 74. For his services as commander of the British squadron, Sir J. Saumarez was made a K.C.B. and awarded a pension of £1,200 per annum.

SYLPH, 28 Sept. 1801. 2 issued. Action with the *Artemise*.

PASLEY, 28 Oct. 1801. 3 issued. Capture of the Spanish ship *Virgen del Rosatio*.

SCORPION, 31 March 1804 (1 issued) and BEAVER, 31 March 1804 (None issued). Action with and capture of vessels in the Ville Road.

CENTURION, 18 Sept. 1804. 11 issued. Action with the line-of-battle ship *Marengo*, and frigates *Atalante* and *Semillante*.

ARROW, 3 Feb. 1805 (8 issued) and ACHERON, 3 Feb. 1805 (2 issued). For the protection of twenty-eight British merchant ships, when attacked by two French frigates.

SAN FIORENZO, 14 Feb. 1805. 11 issued. Capture of the French frigate *Psyche*.

PHOENIX, 10 Aug. 1805. 25 issued. Capture of French frigate *Didon*. This vessel became HMS *Didon*.

TRAFALGAR. 1,710 issued. Thirty-three vessels engaged. A battle which was to see the death of Viscount Nelson and Britain established as indisputable mistress of the seas. The following ships were engaged in the battle: *Victory, Royal Sovereign, Britannia, Conqueror, Temeraire, Neptune, Leviathan, Ajax, Africa, Agamemnon, Minotaur, Orion, Belleisle, Mars, Thunderer, Spartiate, Bellerophon, Achille, Colossus, Polyphemus, Revenge, Dreadnought, Swiftsure, Defence, Defiance, Prince, Naiad*, the frigates, *Sirius, Euryalus. Phoebe*, the cutter, *Entreprenaute* and the schooner, *Pickle*.

4 NOV. 1805. 298 issued. Eight vessels engaged. Capture of four sail of French line-of-battle ships.

ST DOMINGO. 410 issued. Battle of St Domingo, and capture and destruction of four sail of the line. Eleven vessels were engaged.

AMAZON, 13 March 1806 (27 issued) and LONDON, 13 March 1806 (28 issued). Capture of *Marengo* and *Belle Poule*.

PIQUE, 26 March 1806. 7 issued. Capture of the French brigs *Phaeton* and *Voltigeur*.

SIRIUS, 17 April 1806. 12 issued. Action with the French flotilla at Civita Vecchia, and capture of the *Bergere*.

BLANCHE, 19 July 1806. 22 issued. Capture of the *Guerrière*. A knighthood was won by Captain Lavie for this action.

ARETHUSA, 23 Aug. 1806 (6 issued) and ANSON, 23 Aug. 1806. Capture of Spanish frigate *Pomone*.

CURAÇOA, 1 Jan. 1807. Taking of Curaçoa. Four vessels engaged: *Arson, Arethusa, Fisgard* and *Latona*.

PICKLE, 3 Jan. 1807. 1 issued. Capture of the French privateer *La Favorite*.

HYDRA, 6 Aug. 1807. 10 issued. In the harbour of Bergur, *Hydra* attacked the batteries and captured three ships, *L'Eugene, Rosario* and *Caroline*.

COMUS, 15 Aug. 1807. 10 issued. Capture of the Danish frigate *Frederickscoarn*.

LOUISA, 28 Oct. 1807. 1 issued. Action with and defeat of a French privateer.

CARRIER, 4 Nov. 1807. 1 issued. Capture of the French cutter *L'Actif*.

ANN, 24 Nov. 1807. None issued. Action with ten Spanish gunboats.

SAPPHO, 2 March 1808. 5 issued. Capture of the Danish brig *Admiral Yawl*.

SAN FIORENZO, 8 March 1808. 16 issued. Capture of the French frigate *Piedmon-taise*. Captain Hardinge, the British commander was killed in this action and a monument to his memory was erected in St Paul's Cathedral.

EMERALD, 13 March 1808. 12 issued. Destruction of the batteries at Vivero and several war vessels.

CHILDERS, 14 March 1808. 4 issued. Captain Wilson and a crew of sixty-five participated in this action. Skirmish with the Danish brig *Lougen*.

NASSAU, 22 March 1808 (37 issued) and STATELY, 22 March 1808 (25 issued). Destruction of Danish line-of-battle ship *Prince Christian Frederic*. Two ships engaged.

OFF ROTA, 4 April 1808. 20 issued. Fight with gunboats and convoy. *Alceste, Grasshopper* and *Mercury* engaged.

GRASSHOPPER, 24 April 1808 (1 issued) and RAPID, 24 April 1808 (1 issued). Action with and destruction of Spanish ships and gunboats at Faro. Two vessels engaged.

REDWING, 7 May 1808. 7 issued. Action with Spanish gunboats resulting in their destruction.

VIRGINIE, 19 May 1808. 21 issued. Capture of Dutch frigate *Guelderland*.

REDWING, 31 May 1808. 5 issued. Taking of two vessels and destroying Tarifa Battery near Cape Trafalgar.

SEAHORSE with BANDERE LA ZAFFERE, 6 July 1808. 35 issued. Capture of the Turkish frigate *Badere Zaffer*.

COMET, 11 Aug. 1808. 5 issued. Action with three French brigs and the capture of the *Sylphe* which later became HMS *Seagull*.

CENTAUR, 26 Aug. 1808 (38 issued) and IMPLACABLE, 26 Aug. 1808 (45 issued). Fight with Russian fleet and capture of 74-gun ship *Selwolod*.

CRUIZER, 1 Nov. 1808. 4 issued. Action with Danish flotilla off Gottenburgh and the capture of a brig-of-war.

AMETHYST with THETIS, 10 Nov. 1808. 37 issued. Capture of French frigate *Thetis* by Captain Seymour.

OFF THE PEARL ROCK, 13 Dec. 1808. Action with batteries and French boats. Six vessels engaged.

ONYX, 1 Jan. 1809. 6 issued. Recapture from the Dutch of the brig *Manly*.

CONFIANCE, 14 Jan. 1808. 8 issued. Taking of Cayenne.

MARTINIQUE, 523 issued. Capture of Martinique. Forty-three vessels engaged.

HORATIO, 10 Feb. 1809 (14 issued) and SUPÉRIÉURE, 10 Feb. 1809 (2 issued). Capture of the French frigate *Junon*, which joined the Royal Navy under the same name.

AMETHYST, 5 April 1809. 28 issued. Capture of French frigate *Niemen*.

12 APRIL 1809. 646 issued. Engagement with French squadron and destruction of ships in Basque Road. Thirty-five ships participated.

POMPÉE, 17 June 1809 (17 issued), CASTOR, 17 June 1809 (4 issued) and RECRUIT, 17 June 1809 (3 issued). Chase and capture of French ship of the line *Hautpoult*, which later became HMS *Abercromby*. Three vessels engaged. Bars should read April 17 not as listed.

Cyane, 25 and 27 June 1809 (5 issued) and L'ESPOIR, 25 and 27 June 1809 (5 issued). Action with *Ceres*, and the capture of eighteen gunboats, and destruction of four.

BONNE CITOYENNE with FURIEUSE, July 6th 1809. 12 issued. Capture of French frigate *La Furieuse*.

DIANA, 11 Sept. 1809. 3 issued. Capture of Dutch brig *Zephyr*.

ANSE-LE-BARQUE, 18 Dec. 1809. 42 issued. Storming batteries of Anse-le-barque, and capture of *Loire* and *Seine* frigates. Nine vessels engaged.

CHEROKEE, 10 Jan. 1810. 4 issued. Capture of the French lugger *L'Aimable Nelly*.

SCORPION, 12 Jan. 1810. 12 issued. Capture of the French brig *L'Oreste*.

GUADALOUPE, Jan./Feb. 1810. 509 issued. Capture of Guadaloupe. Fifty vessels engaged.

THISTLE, 10 Feb. 1810. None issued. Capture of the Dutch corvette *Havik*.

SURLY, 24 April 1810 (1 issued) and FIRM, 24 April 1810 (1 issued). Capture of the French privateer *Alcide*.

SYLVIA, 26 April 1810. 1 issued. Capture of the Dutch brig *Echo*, in the Straits of Sunda.

SPARTAN, 2 May 1810. 32 issued. Action with the French frigate *Ceres*, and consorts, and capture of the corvette *Sparviéve*.

ROYALIST, May and June 1810. 3 issued. Action in the Channel with and capture of six armed French ships.

AMANTHEA, 25 July 1810. 29 issued. Action with gunboats, and capture and destruction of a number of transports at Amanthea. *Weasel*, *Thames* and *Pilot* engaged.

BANDA NEIRA, 9 Aug. 1810. 69 issued. Three boats engaged. Capture of the Island of Banda Neira.

BOADICEA, 18 Sept. 1810 (16 issued), OTTER, 18 Sept. 1810 (8 issued) and STAUNCH, 18 Sept. 1810 (2 issued). Action with French squadron and capture of the French frigate *Venus* and recapture of the British frigate *Ceylon*. *Otter*, *Staunch* and *Boadicea* engaged. *Venus* joined the Royal Navy as the *Néréide*.

BRISEIS, 14 Oct. 1810. 2 issued. Capture of the French privateer *Sans-Souci*.

LISSA, 13 March 1811. 130 issued. Four vessels engaged in action with a French squadron and capture of frigates off Lissa.

ANHOLT, 27 March 1811. 40 issued. Action in defence of Anholt Island when attacked by Danes.

ARROW, 6 April 1811. None issued. Action with *Chassemarées* and batteries off the French coast.

OFF TAMATAVE, 20 May 1811. 79 issued. Action with French frigates and capture of *Renommée* and *Néréide*. The vessels became HMS *Java* and *Madagascar*. *Racehorse*, *Astree*, *Galatea* and *Phœbe* engaged.

HAWKE, 18 Aug. 1811. 6 issued. Capture of the 16-gun French brig *Heron* and convoy.

JAVA, Aug. & Sept. 1811. 715 issued. Capture of Java. Twenty-five vessels engaged.

SKYLARK, 11 Nov. 1811 (2 issued) and LOCUST, 11 Nov. 1811 (2 issued). Action with Boulogne flotilla of 12 gun-brigs and capture of one.

PELAGOSA, 29 Nov. 1811. 64 issued. Action with French frigates *Pauline* and *Pomone* and capture of same. *Alceste*, *Active* and *Unitie* engaged.

VICTORIOUS with RIVOLI and WEASEL, 22 Feb. 1812 (6 issued). Capture of the French 74 *Rivoli*. The *Victorious* lost twenty-seven killed and ninety-nine wounded, but the *Weasel* did not have a man touched.

ROSARIO, 27 March 1812 (6 issued) and GRIFFON, 27 March 1812 (3 issued). Capture of French brig-of-war off Dieppe. Two vessels engaged.

NORTHUMBERLAND, 22 May 1812 (62 issued) and GROWLER, 22 May 1812 (4 issued). Destruction of the French frigates *Arienne* and *Andromache* plus a brig. Two vessels engaged.

MALAGA, 29 May 1812. 17 issued. Capture of French privateers *Brave* and *Napoleon*, at Malaga. The correct date of this action was in fact 29 April. Four vessels engaged.

OFF MARDOE, 6 July 1812. 48 issued. Destruction of two Danish frigates and two brigs. Four British boats engaged: *Dictator*, *Flamer*, *Calypso* and *Podargus*.

SEALARK, 21 July 1812. 4 issued. Capture of the French privateer *Ville de Caen*.

ROYALIST, 29 Dec. 1812. 3 issued. Capture of the French privateer lugger *La Ruse*.

WEASEL, 22 April 1813. 6 issued. Destruction of six French gunboats in the Adriatic.

SHANNON with CHESAPEAKE, 1 June 1813. 49 issued. Capture of American frigate *Chesapeake*.

PELICAN, 14 Aug. 1813. 4 issued. Capture of the American brig *Argus*.

ST SEBASTIAN, Aug. & Sept. 1813. 292 issued. Sixteen vessels engaged.

THUNDER, 9 Oct. 1813. 7 issued. Capture of the French privateer *Neptune*.

GLUCKSTADT, 5 Jan. 1814. 45 issued. Capture of the fortress of Gluckstadt. Six ships and eight gunboats engaged.

VENERABLE, 16 Jan. 1814 (31 issued) and CYANE, 16 Jan. 1814 (18 issued). Capture of the French frigates *Alcméne* and *Iphigénia*, which were added to the Navy as HMS *Gloire* and *Dunira*.

EUROTAS, 25 Feb. 1814. 32 issued. Capture of the French frigate *Glorinde*, which became HMS *Burma*.

HERBUS with L'ETOILE, 27 March 1814. Capture of the French frigate *L'Etoile*.

PHOEBE, 28 March 1814 (28 issued) and CHERUB, 28 March 1814 (10 issued). Capture of the American frigates *Essex* and *Essex Junior*.

THE POTOMAC, 17 Aug. 1814. 107 issued. Daring navigation of the Potomac River and destruction of shipping in the Potomac. Eight vessels engaged.

ENDYMION with PRESIDENT, 15 Jan. 1815. Capture of the American frigate *President*.

GAIETA, 24 July 1815. 89 issued. Attack and reduction of Gaieta. *Berwick* and *Malta* engaged.

ALGIERS, 27 Aug. 1816. 1,362 issued. Twenty-two vessels engaged.

NAVARINO, 20 Oct. 1827. 1,137 issued. Battle of 'Navarino'. Eleven ships engaged.

SYRIA, Nov. 1840. 6,877 issued. Thirty-two ships engaged. A great number of these were used for fraudulent purposes having rare bars substituted.

Bars granted for boat actions   The boat actions commemorated by these bars cover a number of brilliant actions carried out by boats' crews in cutting out, and in some cases actually recovering, Royal Navy vessels lost to the enemy, or taking and overpowering enemies' vessels.

15 March 1793 (1 issued); 17 March 1794 (30 issued); 29 May 1797 (3 issued); 9 June 1799 (4 issued); 20 Dec. 1799 (3 issued); 29 July 1800 (4 issued); 29 Aug. 1800 (26 issued); 27 Oct. 1800 (5 issued); 21 July 1801 (9 issued); 27 June 1803 (5 issued); 4 Nov. 1803 (1 issued); 4 Feb. 1804 (10 issued); 4 June 1805 (10 issued); 16 July 1806 (51 issued); 2 Jan. 1807 (2 issued); 21 Jan. 1807 (9 issued); 19 April 1807 (1 issued); 13 Feb. 1808 (3 issued); 10 July 1808 (8 issued); 11 Aug. 1808 (12 issued); 28 Nov. 1808 (2 issued); 7 July 1809 (33 issued); 14 July 1809 (8 issued); 25 July 1809 (35 issued); 27 July 1809 (10 issued); 29 July 1809 (11 issued); 28 July 1809 (14 issued); 1 Nov. 1809 (117 issued); 13 Dec. 1809 (10 issued): 13 Feb.

1810 (17 issued); 1 May 1810 (18 issued); 28 June 1810 (24 issued); 27 Sept. 1810 (34 issued); 4 Nov. 1810 (2 issued); 23 Nov. 1810 (66 issued); 24 Dec. 1810 (6 issued); 4 May 1811 (10 issued); 30 July 1811 (4 issued); 2 Aug. 1811 (10 issued); 20 Sept. 1811 (8 issued); 4 Dec. 1811 (18 issued); 4 April 1812 (4 issued); 1 Sept. 1812 and 18 Sept. 1812 (24 issued for these two clasps); 17 Sept. 1812 (11 issued); 29 Sept. 1812 (26 issued); 6 Jan 1812 (21 issued); 21 March 1813 (6 issued); 28 April 1813 (2 issued); April and May 1813 (54 issued); 2 May 1813 (49 issued); 8 April 1814 (23 issued); 24 May 1814 (11 issued); 3 & 6 Sept. 1814 (1 issued); 14 Dec. 1814 (117 issued), the last two bars being awarded for action in the American War.

MILITARY GENERAL SERVICE MEDAL This is the Army equivalent of the NGS and was awarded to men who had seen action between 1793 and 1814. It had a selection of twenty-nine bars: Egypt; Maida; Roleia; Vimiera; Sahagun; Benevente (a single bar, inscribed 'SAHAGUN & BENEVENTE', was awarded to those men who had fought in both engagements); Corunna; Martinique; Talavera; Guadeloupe; Busaco; Barrosa; Fuentes D'Onor; Albuera; Java; Ciudad Rodrigo; Badajoz; Salamanca; Fort Detroit; Chateauguay; Chrystler's Farm; Vittoria; Pyrenees; St Sebastian; Nivelle; Nive; Orthes; Toulouse.
THE CRIMEA 1854–6 Thought to be one of the best designed medals of the Victorian period and struck in sterling silver, the obverse bears the young head of Queen Victoria and the wording, 'VICTORIA REGINA', with the date '1854' beneath the head. The reverse shows a rather striking figure of a Roman warrior armed with a shield and *gladius*. A winged figure of Victory crowns his head with a wreath of laurels. The word 'CRIMEA' is inscribed vertically on the left. The medal was worn from a pale blue ribbon with yellow edges. The bars for this award are in the form of oak leaves with the name of each engagement in the centre. Bars issued are 'INKERMANN', 'ALMA', 'BALAKLAVA', 'SEBASTOPOL' and 'AZOFF', the latter being issued to the Navy for operations in the Sea of Azoff.

In October 1853, the Czar of all the Russias declared war against Turkey. To defend her, Great Britain and France rushed troops to Varna, a Bulgarian port in the Black Sea. At the end of February 1854, Queen Victoria bade farewell to the Guards at Buckingham Palace and these, with other regiments, sailed away to the distant shores of a wild country which was to cost the lives of 21,815, either killed in action or by disease, and 11,876 wounded. Perhaps the most ironic and disturbing statistic reveals that disease alone accounted for 16,041 men, and battle just 4,774.

During the bloody battle of the Alma, the Welsh Fusiliers, who were among the first to land at the Crimea, lost their colonel and eight officers, and the Light Division lost 47 officers and 850 men. The Division was composed of the 7th, 19th, 23rd, 33rd, 77th and the 88th Regiments. The Russians had 5,000 placed *hors de combat*.

57. *Left:* Crimean medal awarded to Samuel Thomas, armourer on *HMS Princess Royal*

58. *Above:* Ashanti medal, 1873–74, with 'Coomassie' bar

The conditions under which men had to live were appalling. While high-ranking officers lived the life of country gentlemen complete with picnic hampers, servants and the whole family on hand, the men and junior officers died like flies in pools of mud and water. Between November 1854 and February 1855, there were 9,000 deaths in hospital, and, by the end of February, there were no less than 13,600 officers and men in hospital. Hospitals were the crudest form of shelter; worn-out bell tents with mud floors and only a meagre ration of meat and weevily biscuits to comfort the wounded. It was in such conditions as these that the 'Lady with the Lamp', Florence Nightingale, tried her best to succour and relieve the pain of the wounded with what little aid was made available to her. This was to be a turning point in British military history. It was only after Miss Nightingale had petitioned for better medical conditions that the Medical Staff Corps was formed in 1855. The Corps became the Army Hospital Corps in 1857, and finally, in 1918, the RAMC.

The best remembered engagement of the whole Crimean campaign must surely be the charge of the Light Brigade in which the Earl of Cardigan and 621 of his men charged the Russian guns. Four hundred and twenty-six of the brigade were placed *hors de combat*; 13 officers and 162 men being killed or taken prisoner and 27 officers and 224 men were wounded. In all, just 195 mounted men struggled back to camp in scattered groups.

Regiments engaged at Balaclava were: the Heavy Brigade, comprising the

59. *Left:* Another colonial war medal, this time for the Zulu-Basuto wars, 1877–79
60. *Right:* Obverse and reverse of the U.S. Congressional Medal of Honor, instituted in December, 1862. This particular medal was awarded to 'First Sergt. William Allen, Co. 1, 23rd U.S. Inf'ty' for action against the Apaches in 1872–73.

1st, 2nd, and 6th Dragoons and 4th and 5th Dragoon Guards; the Light Brigade, consisting of the 13th Light Dragoons and 17th Lancers in the first line, the 4th Light Dragoons, and the 8th and 11th Hussars in the second line, and the 93rd Highlanders. Men in the Rifle Brigades, the Artillery and various line regiments, including the 4th, 19th, 21st, 30th, 33rd, 44th, 47th, 50th, 53rd, 68th, and 77th were all present and received the medal with the bar for Balaclava.

The Crimea medal was issued unnamed, as was its naval counterpart, the Baltic; however, some recipients of the former had their name and regiments engraved privately. Others were officially named later, with the same stamps as were used for the Army General Service and early Kaffir War medals – square Roman capitals.

The bars should read upwards from the medal as follows: 'ALMA'; 'BALA-KLAVA'; 'INKERMANN' and 'SEBASTOPOL'. But, as a number of the medals were issued without the bars being fixed, many are found in the wrong order and in some cases minus the odd bar. Care should be taken to verify the record of the person named on the medal.

The rigmarole of names and places naturally raises the question of renamed pieces. A few years ago Crimea, NGS and MGS medals could be purchased for a few shillings. On some of these bargains, the original name was erased and another stamped over the top. This is not faking as such – it would hardly have been worth

61. Group of U.S. medals won by Colonel A. S. Cummins: *Left to right* Indian campaign medal; Spanish campaign, 1898; Philippine campaign 1899, and First World War Victory Medal

it for the money involved. It seems, however, that hard-up soldiers were in the habit of selling off their medals for beer money. Faced with the problem of parading with his medals on the next full kit inspection, the enterprising soldier 'replaced' the missing articles. Sometimes the 'replaced' medal would have the incriminating name and regiment ground down, leaving the edge rough and blank. Others would slip the storeman a few coppers to stamp in their own regimental details. As years rolled by and the old soldiers faded away, their medals were discarded with the rest of their mementoes to lie unnoticed in junk shops. Now, with the vast interest in all things military, that renamed edge is a cause for much suspicion and research.

Many valuable and rare pieces *are* finding their way onto the market, bearing very high-priced tickets, so it is as well to take that knowledgeable friend along with you if you find a medal that gives some cause for reflection. This also applies to bar rivets and suspender clips, for a number of medals have been 'reborn'. Pretty-looking awards such as the Crimea and India General Service medals were occasionally made into brooches. Cutting off the suspender and clasps, a large pin was usually soldered across the back. Others were drilled at top and bottom edge then mounted gimble fashion. Always check a medal well either for signs of a removed pin, or the two small holes in the edge. In the latter case it has been known for these holes to be plugged with candle wax – a good enough ruse for the uncertain light of market stalls.

The list of collectable medals is almost as long as that of the campaign for which they were awarded. Consult the bibliography for sources of sound information and advice. Why not try to form a collection, therefore, of American Indian Wars medals, as exemplified by the fine collection of George B. Harris III of Colorado.

Alternatively, you could devote your time and energy to the pursuit of medals won by the survivors of the Light Brigade – a life-time's work. Or perhaps a collection of World War 1 'Death Medals' – a large bronze medal having the recipient's name cast into a special space and the three World War 1 medals (Pip, Squeak and Wilfred as they are known in collector's circles), was forwarded to a fallen hero's next-of-kin. I have seen them mounted in a polished wood frame and also let into a garden wall, as a sort of memorial. One collector has formed a rather morbid collection of these huge bronze discs, and faced himself, presumably, with a storage problem – each weighs well over a pound and is 6in in diameter!

A selection of world medals could also form the backbone of a collection, a great number being struck for all manner of reasons or causes. The French St Helena medal of 1857 is a good example. It was over fifty years before a medal was struck by Emperor Napoleon III and awarded to the survivors of the great army who had served under *le petit Caporal* during his campaigns from 1792 to 1815. This oval, bronze medal has on the obverse a beaded circle with laurel leaves, which frame the whole medal and the laureated head of Napoleon facing to the right with the legend 'NAPOLEON I EMPEREUR'. On the reverse, within a beaded circle, is the inscription 'À SES COMPAGNONS DE GLOIRE SA DERNIERE PENSÉE STE. HELENE 5 MAI 1821'. (To his companions in glory his last thought St Helena 5 May 1821), and around, 'CAMPAGNES DE 1792 À 1815', with a small, five-pointed star beneath. The Imperial Crown, above the oval, has a ring affixed to the top through which a 1½in wide ribbon (green with narrow stripes) passes.

The British, for their part glad at long last to be rid of this thorn in their side, had the East India Company issue a halfpenny with the Company's Arms on the obverse, and a laurel wreath enclosing 'ST. HELENA HALFPENNY, 1821', on the reverse. Although the authorities strongly denied the rumours that this coin was nothing more but a rather twisted way of saying farewell to the Emperor, the fact still remains that this was the one and only coin ever to be issued for the island of St Helena.

Cleaning and displaying the collection should be given great consideration. As with any collection of militaria, display is of the utmost importance; many collectors spoil their medals by over-polishing or buffing them up with metal polish. This may be quite satisfactory on the brass or cupro-nickel medals struck for World War 2. Indeed, this is the only sensible course for, unlike their solid silver counterparts of World War 1 and earlier, these cupro-nickel awards cannot be treated in a silver cleanser. However, continual rubbing and polishing of the solid silver medals

62. *Left:* D.S.O. bearing the VRI cypher. 63. *Centre:* Army of India medal awarded to Marine T. Green of *HMS Boadicea*. 58 of his shipmates also received the medal with the 'Ava' clasp. 64. *Right:* Another medal from the far-flung British Empire, this time the Canadian General Service medal, with the Fenian Raid bar, 1866. Awarded to Pte. Benjamin Porier, whose name is on the unofficial brooch buckle

will, in time, reduce them to lumps of polished silver with all their intricate details and highspots reduced to a faceless anonymity.

For the best results when using a silver cleanser, carefully remove the ribbon and place it in between the pages of a heavy book. This ensures that the ribbon is out of harm's way as well as being pressed. When one is handling a ribbon of say, 1860, it pays to be extra careful as, in some instances, the ribbon is harder to acquire than the actual medal! The firms of Hayward or Spinks can usually be relied upon to supply replacement ribbons, but it kills a little of the romance to see an antique piece dolled-up with a brand new shiny ribbon. Now, having stored your ribbon away, thread a thin loop of nylon fishing line through the bar or suspender fitting and thoroughly immerse the medal in the fluid. If two or more are to be treated put them all in at once, leaving the loops of nylon cord hooked over the side of the jar. A word of warning – if the medals are heavily tarnished be sure to carry out the work in a well-ventilated room, workshop or garage. The toxic fumes play havoc with your health. Once the dipped medal takes on a nice brilliant shine, rinse it well in warm, soapy water and, after drying on a soft piece of towelling, lightly polish it with a 'Long Term' or similar silver cloth.

Ribbons can pose problems, especially if they are of any great age. Many of those issued at about the turn of the century prove no trouble to replace but those of, say, Germany or Italy 1939–45 or any pre-1860 examples are rather more difficult to find. With these very old ribbons, the only recourse is to lightly press them with a warm iron, using a cloth or brown paper as a barrier. Preserve them at all costs – a frayed, battered piece of antique ribbon is better than no ribbon at all.

Once the collection tops a dozen, the problem of suitable presentation arises. Many collectors display their medals in a ready-made cabinet comprised of thin, tray-like drawers lined with green baize. Although this is handy for the collector faced with a space shortage, some collectors prefer to display medals in glazed frames. This rather effective and picturesque way of showing war medals is most rewarding for, with the many and various combinations of ribbon colours, the whole display can be a beautiful adornment to a room. Frames can be made to a specific size or purchased from second-hand shops.

If the picture frame method of display is to be used, the medals should be firmly fixed to the backing. Nothing is worse than having a good collection of EF to UNC (Extremely Fine and Uncirculated) items, shaken off their backing and scattered all around the room. Peg-board is by far the favourite method as it can be purchased in small off-cuts. The ready punched holes spaced 1in or $\frac{1}{2}$in apart make it much easier to sew the ribbons to the velvet and then through into the holes behind. Press pins can be used of course in all instances but, unless you purchase all-brass pins, the medals are liable to pick up a certain amount of rust on the ribbon from the inferior brass-coated or steel variety. If you do decide to use press pins be sure to mount the medal carefully. Failure to do so makes for an unsightly pin-head on all the ribbons displayed. Take each medal to be displayed and lay it in position. Gently flip it on its back, stretching the medal out to its full length of ribbon. Press in the pin about $\frac{1}{2}$in from the ribbon end and then return the medal to its proper position by bringing the ribbon right over the pin-head, thus concealing it from view.

For a safer, neater and more professional touch I recommend sewing them through the velvet and onto the peg-board holes. Once the medals are correctly in position and the small identification labels installed, finish the display off by pasting a piece of thick brown paper over the back of the frame. This effectively combats the ever-present danger of dust filtering in through the back, and damaging both ribbons and medals.

Appendix – Military Museums and Collections

Although most of these are open to the general public, it is advisable to write in advance to confirm times of viewing.

General

Enfield Pattern Room, Royal Small Arms Factory, Enfield Lock, Enfield, Middx. (by special permission only).

H.M. Tower Armouries, Tower of London, Tower Hill, London E.C.3.

Imperial War Museum, Lambeth Rd., London S.E.1.

National Maritime Museum, Greenwich, London S.E.10.

Preston Hall Museum of Social History (fine collection of early weapons dating from the sixteenth century), Yarm Road, Eaglescliffe, near Stockton, Durham.

Public Records Office, Chancery Lane, London W.C.2.

Scottish United Services Museum, Crown Square, The Castle, Edinburgh 1.

Victoria & Albert Museum, Cromwell Road, London S.W.7.

Wellington Museum, Apsley House, 149 Piccadilly, London W.1.

Services Museums

ROYAL NAVY

Fleet Air Arm Museum, R.N.A.S. Yeovilton, near Ilchester, Somerset.

Royal Marines Museum, R.M. Barracks, Eastney, Portsmouth, Hants.

Submarine Museum, H.M.S. Dolphin, Gosport, Hants.

Victory Museum, H.M. Dockyard, Portsmouth, Hants.

ARMY

Airborne Forces Museum, Browning Barracks, Aldershot, Hants.

Army Aviation Museum, Middle Wallop, Hants.

Dorset Military Museum, The Keep, Dorchester, Dorset.

Museum of Artillery, The Rotunda, Woolwich, London S.E.18.

National Army Museum, Royal Hospital Road, London S.W.3.

School of Infantry Museum, School of Infantry, Warminster, Wilts.

Scottish Infantry Depot (Glencorse) Museum, Glencorse Barracks, Milton Bridge, Penicuik, Midlothian.

Welsh Brigade Museum, Cwyt-y-gollen, Crickhowell, near Abergavenny, Monmouthshire.

ROYAL AIR FORCE
Royal Air Force Museum, (R.E. Balloonists) R.F.C., R.N.A.S., R.A.F. Hendon.
Shuttleworth (historical aircraft) Collection, Old Warden Aerodrome, Biggleswade, Beds.

Regimental and Corps Museums

Argyll and Sutherland Highlanders Regimental Museum, The Castle, Stirling, Scotland.
Army Catering Corps, RHQ St., Omer Barracks, Aldershot, Hants.
Army Physical Training Corps Museum, Corps Depot, Queen's Avenue, Aldershot.
Ayrshire Yeomanry Museum, Yeomanry House, Chalmers Rd, Ayr.
Berkshire & Westminster Dragoons Museum, RHQ, 1, Elverton St, Horseferry Road, London S.W.1.
Black Watch Museum, Balhousie Castle, Perth, Scotland.
Border Regiment Museum, The Keep, The Castle, Carlisle, Cumberland.
Buffs Regimental Museum, Poor Priests Hospital, Stour St, Canterbury, Kent.
Cameronians (Scottish Rifles) Regimental Museum, 129, Muir St, Hamilton, Lanarkshire.
3rd Carabiniers (Prince of Wales' Dragoon Guards) Regimental Museum, The Castle, Chester, Cheshire.
22nd (Cheshire) Regiment Museum, The Castle, Chester, Cheshire.
Corps of Royal Engineers, Museum of, Brompton Barracks, Chatham, Kent.
Devonshire Regiment Museum, Wyvern Barracks, Exeter, Devonshire.
Duke of Cornwall's Light Infantry Regimental Museum, The Keep, The Barracks, Bodmin, Cornwall.
East Lancashire Regiment Museum, Blackburn Museum, Blackburn, Lancs.
East Lancashire Regiment, Towneley Hall Art Gallery & Museum, Burnley, Lancs.
Essex Regiment Museum, Oaklands Park, Chelmsford, Essex.
Gloucestershire Regiment, Museum of, Bishop Hooper's Lodging, 99–103, Westgate St, Gloucester.
Gordon Highlanders Museum, Viewfield Rd, Aberdeen, Scotland.
Green Howards Museum, Gallowgate, Richmond, Yorkshire.
Guards Museum, Wellington Barracks, Birdcage Walk, London S.W.1.
Hereford Light Infantry (Territorial) Museum, TA Centre, Harold St, Hereford, Herts.
Honourable Artillery Company, Armoury Rd, City Rd, by Finsbury Sq, London E.C.1.
Household Cavalry Museum, (1st & 2nd Life Guards, Horse Grenadier Guards, The Life Guards, Royal Horse Guards (The Blues), 1st Royal Dragoons), Combermere Barracks, Windsor, Berks.
Intelligence Corps Museum, Temper Barracks, Ashford, Kent.
Irish Cavalry Regiments (5th Royal Inniskilling Dragoon Guards, Queen's Royal Irish Hussars, North Irish Horse), Museum of, Carrickfergus, Co. Antrim.
Kent & County of London Yeomanry (Sharpshooters), Squerryes Court, Westerham. (Correspondence pertaining to this regiment to: OC (KCLY) Squadron, Royal Yeomanry Regt, TAVR Centre, Mitcham Rd, Croydon, Surrey.
King's Own (Lancaster) Regimental Museum, Old Town Hall, Market Square, Lancaster, Lancashire.

King's Own Scottish Borderers Regimental Museum, The Barracks, Berwick upon Tweed, Northumberland.

King's Own Yorkshire Light Infantry Regimental Museum, Wakefield Rd, Pontefract, Yorks.

King's Regiment (Liverpool) City of Liverpool Museum, William Brown St, Liverpool L3 8EN.

15th/19th The King's Royal Hussars, Hutton Terrace, Sandyford Rd, Newcastle NE2 1SH, Northumberland.

King's Shropshire Light Infantry and the Hereford Light Infantry Museum, Sir John Moore Barracks, Copthorne, Shrewsbury, Shropshire.

King's Shropshire Light Infantry (Territorial) Museum, The Drill Hall, Goleham, Shrewsbury, Shropshire.

Lancashire Fusiliers, Regimental Museum of, Wellington Barracks, Bury, Lancs.

17th/21st Lancers Regimental Museum, Belvoir Castle, near Grantham, Lancs.

Light Infantry Museum, Sir John Moore Barracks, Copthorne, Shrewsbury, Shropshire.

London Irish Rifles Regimental Museum, Duke of York's HQ, King's Rd, London S.W.3.

London Scottish Regimental Museum, 59, Buckingham Gate, London S.W.3.

Manchester Regiment & 14th/20th King's Hussars Museum, Queen's Park, Harpurhey, Manchester 9, Lancs.

Middlesex Regimental Museum, Bruce Castle, Lordship Lane, Tottenham, London.

Northamptonshire Regiment, Abington Park Museum, Abington, Northampton.

Prince of Wales' Own Regiment of Yorkshire Museum, Imphal Barracks, Fulford, Yorks.

Queen Alexandra's Royal Army Nursing Corps, Training Centre, Royal Pavilion, Farnborough Rd, Aldershot, Hants.

1st The Queen's Dragoon Guards Regimental Museum, Clive House, College Hill, Shrewsbury, Shropshire.

Queen's Lancashire Regiment (incorporating The Loyal Regt, 2nd, 47th and 81st Foot), Fulwood Barracks, Watling St, Preston, Lancs.

Queen's Own Hussars Museum, The Lord Leycester Hospital, High St, Warwick.

Queen's Own Royal West Kent Museum, The Maidstone Museum and Art Gallery, St Faith's St, Maidstone, Kent.

Queen's Own Warwickshire & Worcestershire Yeomanry Regimental Museum, Drill Hall, New Broad St, Stratford, Warwickshire.

Queen's Regimental Museum, (Middlesex, Queen's Surreys, Royal Sussex, Queen's Own Buffs Regiments) R.H.Q., The Queen's Regiment, Howe Barracks, Canterbury, Kent.

Queen's Royal Surrey Regiment, Museum of, Surbiton Rd, Kingston, Surrey.

Royal Armoured Corps Tank Museum, & Royal Tank Regiment Museum, Bovington Camp, Wareham, Dorset.

Royal Army Chaplain's Department, Museum of, Bagshot Park, Surrey.

Royal Army Dental Corps Museum, RADC Training Centre, Connaught Barracks, Duke of Connaught's Rd, Aldershot, Hants.

Royal Army Educational Corps Museum, RAEC Centre, Wilton Park, Beaconsfield, Bucks.

Royal Army Medical Corps Historical Museum, Keogh Barracks, Ash Vale, Aldershot, Hants.

Royal Army Ordnance Corps Museum, RAOC Training Centre, Deepcut, Camberley, Surrey.

Royal Army Pay Corps Museum, Worthy Down, Winchester, Hampshire.

Royal Army Veterinary Corps Museum, RAVC School, Thornhill, Aldershot.

Royal Berkshire Regiment Museum, Brock Barracks, Oxford Rd, Reading.

Royal Corps of Transport Railway Model Room and Museum, Army School of Transport, Longmoor Camp, Liss, Hants.

Royal Corps of Transport, Regimental Museum, HQ Training Centre, RCT, Buller Barracks, Aldershot, Hants.

4th/7th Royal Dragoon Guards Museum, Bankfield Museum, Haley Hill, Halifax, Yorks.

Royal Electrical and Mechanical Engineers Museum, Moat House, Aberfield, Reading, Berkshire.

Royal Fusiliers Museum, H.M. Tower of London, London E.C.3.

Royal Green Jackets Museum, Peninsula Barracks, Romsey Rd, Winchester, Hants.

Royal Hampshire Regiment Museum, Searle's House, Southgate St, Winchester, Hampshire.

Royal Highland Fusiliers Museum, 518, Sauchiehall St, Glasgow C.2.

13th/18th Royal Hussars (The Lilywhite's), Cannon Hall, Cawthorne, Barnsley, Yorks.

Royal Inniskilling Fusiliers, Regimental Museum of, The Castle, Enniskillen, Co. Fermanagh.

Royal Irish Fusiliers, Regimental Museum, Sovereign's House, The Mall, Armagh.

Royal Leicestershire Regimental Museum, Magazine Tower, The Newarke, Oxford St, Leicester.

Royal Lincolnshire Regiment, Museum of, The Keep, Sobraon Barracks, Burton Rd, Lincoln, Lincs.

Royal Military Police Museum, Roussillon Barracks, Chichester, Sussex.

Royal Norfolk Regimental Museum, Britannia Barracks, Norwich, Norfolk.

Royal Northumberland Fusiliers Regimental Museum, The Abbot's Tower, Alnwick Castle, Northumberland.

Royal Pioneer Corps Museum, Corps H.Q., Simpson Barracks, Wooton, Northampton NN4 0HX, Northants.

Royal Scots Greys, The Royal Scots Greys' Room, Scottish United Services Museum, The Castle, Edinburgh 1, Scotland.

Royal Scots Regimental Museum, RHQ, The Castle, Edinburgh 1, Scotland.

Royal Signals Museum, Blandford Camp, Blandford Forum, Dorset.

Royal Sussex Regiment Museum, Chichester City Museum, 29, Little London, Chichester, Sussex.

Royal Ulster Rifles, (Royal Irish Rangers), 5, Waring St, Belfast.

Royal Warwickshire Regimental Museum, St John's House, Warwick.

Royal Welch Fusiliers Regimental Museum, The Queen's Tower, Caernarvon Castle, Caernarvon, Wales.

Scottish Horse Museum, The Cross, Dunkeld, Perthshire, Scotland.

Seaforth Highlanders, The Queen's Own Cameron Highlanders, and Queen's Own Highlanders (Seaforth & Camerons), Regimental Museum of, Fort George, Inverness-shire.

Sherwood Foresters, Nottingham and Derbyshire Museum, The Castle, Nottingham.

Shropshire Yeomanry and Shropshire RHA Museum, Territorial House, Sundorne Rd, Shrewsbury, Shropshire.

Somerset Light Infantry Military Museum, 14, Mount St, Taunton, Somerset.

South Lancashire Regiment (PWV) Peninsula Barracks, Warrington, Lancs.

South Wales Borders & Monmouthshire Regiments, Regimental Museum, The Barracks, Brecon, Wales.

21st Special Air Service Regiment (Artists) Museum, B Block, Duke of York's HQ, King's Rd, London S.W.3.

Staffordshire Regimental Museum, Whittington Barracks, Lichfield, Staffs.

Suffolk Regiment Museum, (also Cambridgeshire Regiment TA), The Keep, Gibraltar Barracks, Bury St Edmunds, Suffolk.

Welch Regiment, Regiment Museum, The Barracks, Whitechurch Rd, Cardiff, Glamorgan.

Wiltshire Regiment Museum, Le Marchant Barracks, Devizes, Wiltshire.

Women's Royal Army Corps Museum (ATS, WRAC, QMAAC, WAAC), WRAC Centre, Queen Elizabeth Park, Guildford, Surrey.

Worcestershire Regimental Museum, Worcester City Museum, Foregate St, Worcester.

York and Lancaster Regiment, Regimental Museum, Endcliffe Hall, Endcliffe Vale Rd, Sheffield S10 3EU, Yorks.

Yorkshire Regiments Museum (East & West Yorkshire Regiments, Prince of Wales Own, York & Lancaster Regiment, The Duke of Wellington's Regiment), Queen Elizabeth Barracks, Strensall, Yorks.

Yorkshire regiments, military collection of, Castle Museum, York.

For those interested in Nazi equipment and regalia, a visit to Jersey will be most rewarding.

German Military Underground Hospital, St Lawrence, Jersey (The galleries are set out with relics of the occupation).

Museum of Nazi German Equipment and Occupation Relics, St Peter's Bunker, Jersey.

Hougue Bie Museum, Five Oaks, ($3\frac{1}{2}$ miles from St Helier).

Bibliography

Barnes, Major R. M. *Military Uniforms of Britain and the Empire 1742 to the Present Time* (London, 1960)

Blackmore, H. L. *British Military Firearms* (London, 1961)

Carman, W. J. *Indian Army Uniforms under the British from 18th Century, Cavalry* (London, 1961)

Congreve, William. *An Elementary Treatise on the Mounting of Naval Ordnance 1811* (London, 1970)

Garratt, J. G. *Model Soldiers, a Collector's Guide* (1971)

Gaylor, J. *Military Badge Collecting* (London, 1971)

Gordon, Major L. L. *British Orders and Awards* (London, 1968)

——. *British Battles & Medals* (London, 1971)

Hieronymussen, Paul. *Orders, Medals and Decorations of Britain and Europe* (1967)

Kerrigan, E. E. *American Badges and Insignia* (London, 1971)

Latham, John Wilkinson. *British Military Swords from 1800 to the Present Day* (London, 1966)

Littlejohn, David & Dodkins, Col. C. M. *Orders, Decorations, Medals, and Badges of the Third Reich* (USA, 1968)

Mackenzie, Col. R. H. *The Trafalgar Roll* (reprinted 1970)

Mollo, A. *Daggers of the Third German Reich, 1933–1945*

Mollo, J. *Uniforms of the SS* Vol. 1

Robinson, Russell H. *Oriental Armour* (London, 1967)

Peterson, H. L. *Daggers & Fighting Knives of the Western World* (1968)

Santoro, Cesare. *Hitler's Germany* (Berlin, 1938)

Smyth, Sir John. *Story of the Victoria Cross, 1856–64*

Stephens, F. J. *The Collector's Pictorial Book of Bayonets* (London, 1971)

Index